WORD PROCESSING ASSIGNMENTS

Elementary to Advanced

(Second Edition)

MARY WADE

GILL & MACMILLAN

Gill & Macmillan Ltd
Hume Avenue
Park West
Dublin 12
with associated companies throughout the world
www.gillmacmillan.ie

0 7171 3201 3

Print origination in Ireland by Paradigm Publishing Services

The paper used in this book is made from the wood pulp of managed forests. For every tree felled, at least one tree is planted, thereby renewing natural resources.

For Bill, Willie, Gary and Ronan

CONTENTS

Section Two: ADDITIONAL WORD PROCESSING TECHNIQUES

PREFACE

Word Processing Assignments — Second Edition — is designed for Elementary to Advanced word processing users. This edition contains more 'user-friendly' assignments, particularly in Section 1. It now features many new word processing areas included with the syllabi of the NCVA Word Processing Level 2 and Advanced Practical Exams in mind. It can also be used in the preparation for any word processing examination.

This book is not a tutorial but complements the comprehensive documentation that accompanies all word processing software. It can be used with any word processing package, such as Word for Windows, WordPerfect for Windows and AmiPro.

The material is organised as a series of graduated examples. The topics are presented in a recommended order, but, obviously, a teacher's experience and discretion might dictate sequence and/or assignment reduction. The detailed contents pages easily facilitate any selection.

The topic is outlined and general word processing guidelines are given at the beginning of each Unit. Students should consult the guide to proofreading symbols for clarification of correction signs, and the comprehensive glossary at the back of the book for clear definitions of word processing terminology.

To get the most out of this book, the novice word processing operator should work through the exercises at the computer. The student will quickly master the basics of word processing and develop the confidence to explore additional techniques.

PROOFREADING SYMBOLS

λ	Caret — insert letter or word(s)	λ	is placed where the insertion is to be made
or del	Delete	/	through letter(s) or word(s)
NP or ||	New paragraph	[	placed before the first word of a new paragraph
Run on	No new paragraph required		
l/c or lc/	Lower case = small letter(s)	– /	under letter(s) to be modified or struck through letter(s)
u/c or uc/ or Caps	Upper case = capital letter(s)	=	under letter(s) to be modified or struck through letter(s)
Stet	Let it stand, i.e. type the word(s) that have been crossed out and have a dotted or broken line underneath	......	under word(s) struck out
#	Insert space	λ	
⌒	Close up — less space	⌒	

SECTION ONE

Elementary

Widow	The first line of a paragraph of text that is separated from the rest of the paragraph. A widow line appears at the bottom of the page, whereas the rest of the paragraph appears at the top of the next page.
Wildcards	Characters or symbols used in place of a number of possible combinations. Wildcards represent one or more characters that 'could be anything' in a search or command.
Window	A window is a viewport (outline through which you see) on the screen that displays data, programs or information. A window can be moved, resized, opened and closed allowing you to organise the data on your computer screen.
Windows	Short for Microsoft Windows, a graphical user interface for DOS computers. Microsoft Windows provides a common way of using programs, making them easier to learn. Plus, Windows manages the way your PC works and takes care of common chores, such as working with the printer and disk drive.
Word Processor	An application that lets you write and edit documents. Word processors generally include the capability to copy and move text, search for specific words or phrases, insert and delete text, format the document (including margin settings, fonts, and character styles) and print the document. Popular word processors include Microsoft Word, WordPerfect and AmiPro.
Word Wrap	Word wrap refers to the way a word processor automatically determines whether the word you are typing will fit within the right margin and, if not, places that word on the next line. With word wrap, you don't have to press the Enter key at the end of each line, as you once had to do with a typewriter.
Write Protect	To modify a disk or file so it's unwilling and unable to edit or erase its data.
Zap	To zap a file is to remove it permanently from the disk.

Unit 1

Loading Word Processing Software

Keying in a Document

Inserting Text

Opening a Document

Proofreading

Saving

Closing a File

Exiting from Software

Exiting from the Computer System

Title Bar	This is the title that is prominently displayed in a long bar that stretches across the whole Window. It typically includes the name of both the application you're using and the document you're working in. Even when you haven't named the new file yet, the program will provisionally give the document a name.
Toggle	A type of switch that alternates between two modes, on or off. In a computer program, a toggle may be a graphical button or some other option that can be either on or off. Selecting the button once turns it on, again turns it off.
Toner Cartridge	A cartridge, or container, for a laser printer that holds the toner.
Toolbox	For software users, a collection of tools that serve a common purpose. (See Tools.)
Tools	A set of electronic 'tools' that you can use within a given software application which have effects like the real-life tools they're named after, e.g. you have 'brushes' in a paint program.
Touch Pad	An input device for which all you need to do is touch a spot and it will register as a signal to the computer.
Tractor Feed	A mechanism for feeding paper through dot-matrix printers.
Typeface	The design of characters in a font. Typeface refers to the physical characteristics of a family of letters and numbers. The main division between the categories of typefaces lies in their use of serifs.
Undelete	To put something back the way it was before you deleted it.
Underline	In word processing, the attribute applies to text that makes it look underlined.
Undo	The command in most applications that enables you to cancel the effects of whatever you just did.
Up Arrow	An arrow pointing upward, as found on one of your Cursor Movement keys. Pushing the Up Arrow key moves the cursor up in the document by one line of text.
Upper	On a PC, this term refers to the portion of memory not used by DOS for running Memory programs.
User Friendly	It means you can easily figure out what to do without having to look it up in the manual or the on-line help.
Utility	Software intended to help you fix or enhance your system. Utilities are designed to make working with the computer or your operating system easier.
Variable	In programming, a symbol that represents a numerical value or string of text used in the program. In mail merge, it applies to data that changes from one field to the next.
Vertical Scroll Bar	The bar on the right side of a window in a graphical application. By clicking the scroll bar with your mouse or using the arrow keys, you can move the contents of the window up or down in various increments.
VGA	Acronym for Video Graphics Array. It is a colour graphics display standard. A VGA monitor can display up to 256 colours at one time.
Volatile Memory	See RAM.

Guidelines

1. Loading Word Processing Software

Follow the manufacturer's steps for turning on the word processing software. For example, Word for Windows is turned on by clicking the Start button on the Desktop, then selecting Programs from the Menu, followed by clicking on Word for Windows — a blank document opens on screen in readiness for the inputting of material.

2. Keying in a Document

The cursor is flashing in the open document. Type into the open document; the default (see Glossary) margins control the amount of text that fits onto a line. The wrapround facility (see word wrap in Glossary) automatically wraps text around to the next line. Two spaces must be inserted after a full stop at the end of a sentence. The Return key is hit twice between paragraphs thereby creating a clear line.

3. Inserting Text

Use the Cursor Movement keys (or the mouse) to move the cursor. With the cursor in position, key in the text in the specified positions.

4. Opening a Document

Use the File Open command for your word processing software to recall a document to the screen.

5. Proofreading

Students should read carefully through the typed exercise. Use the Cursor Movement keys (or the mouse) to move the cursor around. Use the Delete key or Backspace key to correct errors and retype.

6. Saving

Text is held in memory (see RAM in Glossary) temporarily. If the power is turned off, it is lost. It is very important to save regularly — at least once every five minutes.

7. Closing a File

Remove the open document from the screen (and memory) by using the File Close command of your word processing software.

8. Exiting from Software

Close down word processing software by using the software's Exit command.

9. Exiting from the Computer System

Close down the system by using the Shut Down command. Turn off the computer.

Space Bar	The longest key on your keyboard; the one that produces the space character.
Space Character	The character, or blank, produced by pressing the space bar.
Spell Checker	A program, usually built-in to a word processor, that examines every word you've typed for correct spelling and offers possible corrections when it finds a word it doesn't recognise.
Spool	To store data temporarily before printing it.
Spooler	Memory that's either built-in to a printer, carved out from the computer's main memory, or stored in a separate box connected between a printer and a computer.
Start-Up Disk	The floppy or hard disk that the computer uses when you turn it on for the first time.
Storage	A place to put valuable information. Common storage devices are tape drives, floppy disks, hard disks, and CD-ROM disks.
Style	Text formatting and character attributes all combined into one. Style refers to the way text looks. In some programs, you can format your text using a STYLE command.
Stylus	The stylus is a type of input device like a mouse.
System Disk	A disk that contains the system, or all the programs required to start a computer.
Subdirectory	A directory within or 'under' the current directory. All disks have directories in which they store files. The directories can also store other directories, which are then called subdirectories.
Subscript	Text that appears smaller and below the surrounding text. Subscript is a text formatting attribute available in word processors and other programs that lets you manipulate text.
Superscript	Text that appears smaller and above the surrounding text.
System Disk	A disk that contains the system, or all the programs required to start your computer. The system disk is usually the hard drive, which starts the computer each time it is turned on.
Tab	Blank spaces created by pressing the Tab key. These spaces are treated as a single unit, so if, for example, if you delete the tab space, you delete the whole thing, not one blank character at a time.
Tab Key	The key on the keyboard that produces the tab 'character'. Pressing the Tab key moves you forward one tab stop.
Table	A way of organising data or text into rows and columns.
Terminal	A monitor hooked up to a mainframe computer.
Text	Letters, numbers, and other characters or symbols found on your keyboard.
Text Box	A box on the screen, outlining an area in which you can type text.
Thesaurus	This is a collection of words and other words with the same meaning. In computers, it refers to the capability of a word processing program to come up with synonyms to match a word you've chosen. You can highlight a word, ask the thesaurus for some synonyms, and the software generates a list of alternatives or suggestions.

TASK 1A

- Key in the following exercise.
- Proofread carefully. Use the Backspace key to delete any errors and retype.
- Save under the combined filename 'Task 1A' and your initials, e.g. 'Task 1A MW'.
- Close file.

Keen decorators Nicola couldn't believe their luck when they first laid eyes on their home. While the back of it has a cosy, cottage-style feel to it, the facade is elegantly Georgian, and with a track record of properties - the couple previously lived in a two-storey clock tower - they fell for their new home's split personality. "As soon as we had a look round, we could see how much potential it had", says Nicola. "I have always loved doing up properties, although I have a sneaking suspicion that Simon prefers it once all the work is over". Nicola immediately set to work, planning new colour schemes. "I have to admit that Nicola does all the work", says Simon. "She hangs up fabric samples and looks at them before making a decision, but it always looks good".

Scroll Bar	A horizontal or vertical rectangular strip that often appears at the right and bottom sides of windows. The scroll bar lets you use a mouse to scroll the image up/down or left/right. The scroll bar also shows you the approximate position of the current screen in relation to the beginning or end of the file.
Search	To examine a file for specific data such as words, characters or symbols.
Search and Replace	To look for specific characters in a file and substitute them for another character or group of characters. Every word processor offers a SEARCH AND REPLACE command so that you can quickly change multiple words or phrases at the touch of a button.
Sector	To store data, disks are formatted into concentric rings called tracks and each track is further divided into sectors.
Segment	In the PC, a segment refers to a 64K block of memory.
Select	To highlight and choose text or graphics that appear on screen, usually by dragging the mouse using the Cursor keys.
Select All	To highlight and choose all text and graphic images on-screen or in your document at one time. It is a useful command to use to erase everything at once, adjust everything on-screen, or copy everything at the same time.
Selected	Highlighted text or graphic images that show you what objects will be affected by the next command you give (e.g. cut, copy, delete).
Sequential Access	To scan information starting from the beginning, such as a tape backup. In comparison, random access lets you scan for information anywhere, such as on a CD-ROM disk.
Serif	Tiny ornamental curves on letters to make them easier to read. Most typefaces have serifs.
Setup	The modification of a program or computer so it works in a particular way each time you use it. The first time you set up a program or computer is when you install it. Later, you can adjust the settings.
Sheet Feeder	A tray that holds paper and feeds it one page or a sheet at a time to a printer. Sheet feeders let you use special stationery or letterheads.
Shift Key	The key labelled Shift that you have to hold down to produce upper-case letters. The Shift key can also be used with function keys for commands, such as Shift F4.
Show Clipboard	A command that lets you see the last item that was cut or copied from the screen. By choosing the SHOW CLIPBOARD command first, you can see what will appear on-screen if you choose the PASTE command next.
Single Density	The earliest form of storage on magnetic media that has been replaced with double-density and high-density. A single-density 5.25" floppy disk might contain 180K of data, a double-density 5.25" floppy disk might contain 360K, and a high-density 5.25" floppy disk might hold 1.2 MB.
Single Sided Disk	A floppy disk that stores data only on one side.
Small Caps	A text attribute or style where lower-case letters are replaced by capital letters of a smaller size.
Software	Computer programs software generally refers to any type of computer programs, from an operating system such as DOS, to a utility, to an application, to a program stored on a ROM chip. This contrasts with hardware, which is the physical side of computing. It's the software that makes the hardware go.
Sort	To organise according to some pattern or rule. The typical sort is alphabetical, though you can also have numeric sorts. Sorts can also be ascending or descending. An ascending sort is from first to last, smallest to biggest, or A to Z. Descending goes the other way.

TASK 1B

- Open the file saved as 'Task 1A MW'.
- Insert the handwritten text at the points indicated.
- Proofread carefully and save as 'Task 1B MW' — the file with additional text will overwrite the existing file.
- Close the file.

Keen decorators Nicola [Cambridgeshire] [and Simon] couldn't believe their luck when they first laid eyes on [and their two sons] their home. While the back of it has a cosy, cottage-style feel to it, the facade is elegantly Georgian, and with a track record of properties - the couple [unusual] previously lived in a two-storey clock tower - they fell for their new home's split personality. "As soon as we had a look round, we could see how much potential it had", says Nicola. "I have always loved doing up properties, although I have a sneaking suspicion that Simon prefers it once all the work is [hard] over". Nicola immediately set to work, planning new colour schemes. "I have to admit that Nicola does all the work", says Simon. "She hangs up fabric samples and looks at them before making a decision, but it always looks good". [in the end] [for weeks]

Queue	A collection of documents or files waiting in turn for printing or some other form of processing.
Quit	A command that exits a program.
Qwerty	The name commonly given to a standard keyboard layout.

Ragged Justification	Text that has an uneven right edge.
RAM	Random Access Memory is a type of computer memory that can be written to and read from.
Random Access	The ability to access any piece of information from a storage medium, such as a disk or RAM.
Read	The act of transferring data from a storage medium to the internal RAM of a computer. The computer 'reads' information from a disk and then stores it into memory.
Read Only	A type of medium from which you can read data but not write data to it. CD-ROM disks are read only media.
Record	An individual unit of data stored in a database. A record consists of one or more related fields, which are the actual pieces of data being stored.
Read/Write Head	The mechanism in a disk drive that accesses and stores information on the disk.
Retrieve	To retrieve a file means to open a file.
Return Key	Same as the Enter key, but it gets its name from the carriage return key on a typewriter.
ROM	Acronym for Read-Only Memory. ROM is any type of memory that can be read but not written to.
Roman	A classification of type styles (fonts), including Times and many others.
Root Directory	The first and often only directory on a disk. The root directory doesn't become important until you have subdirectories and a disk tree structure, then the other directories — the subdirectories — branch from the root like a tree. In DOS, the symbol for the root directory is the single backslash.
Row	A horizontal array of data, as in a spreadsheet or table. Spreadsheets organise data into rows and columns to make totals and other calculations faster and easier. The row may also refer to a line of text in a word processing document or just a line of text across the screen.

Sans Serif	A typeface that lacks serifs, which are tiny ornamental curves that appear at the edges of letters.
Save	To store data (from RAM) on to a floppy or hard disk.
Save As	To store an existing file under a different name. The SAVE AS command saves a file, but it allows you to change the filename.
Scaleable Font	A type font that can appear in different sizes.
Screen Buffer	An area of memory used to store the graphic or text image displayed on-screen.
Screen Dump	A printout of the image that appears on-screen.
Screen Font	A bit-mapped font that mimics the appearance of printer fonts.
Scroll	To move text or graphics vertically or horizontally on-screen.

TASK 1C

- Key in the following exercise.
- Proofread carefully. Use the Backspace key to delete any errors and retype.
- Save under the combined filename 'Task 1C' and your initials, e.g. 'Task 1C MW'.
- Close the file.

The first room was the kitchen - and they certainly had their work. "When we arrived it was in a dreadful state," says Simon. "One wall was covered in woodchip and the sink was at the wrong end of the room, so we moved it to overlook the window." Nicola felt sure there was something behind the brick arch in the kitchen but after Simon warned her not to go in case she unearthed any wires, she got the builders to do it instead. And her instincts were right - they uncovered an original bread oven and an inglenook fireplace, which now contains their Rangemaster cooker. The kitchen now has a classic farmhouse feel thanks to the colours Nicola has used.

Page Down Key	A cursor key that moves you forward in the document the exact length of a page every time you press it.
Page Up Key	The opposite of the Page Down key.
Pagination	The act of making pages where there were none.
Paint	Paint programs give you tools that let you draw electronically on the computer screen for different effects, e.g different size brushes, roller (for larger areas), a spray can.
Palette	The selection of colours available in a paint or drawing program.
Pane	A portion of a window that has been split into multiple parts.
Parameters	A value — which could be numbers, letters, or other characters — that you enter into an equation or statement, like an option.
Parity Bit	An extra bit included to check the parity in data bytes. The arrangement is specified, say, that a parity bit set to 1 means that the parity is odd, 0 if it is even.
Password	Usually found in a computer network, where a password is required to access certain parts of the network.
Paste	To insert an item previously cut or copied from elsewhere.
Pentium	A brand new chip (microprocessor) for personal computers, manufactured by Intel. It is the successor to the 486 chip. Intel was going to call this the 586 chip but they couldn't copyright the term, so they called it the Pentium.
Peripheral	Any machinery connected to the computer, including monitors, printer, scanners, mice, external hard or floppy drives.
Permanent Storage	Hard drives, floppy drives and ROM are examples of permanent storage. RAM is the opposite.
Pica	One pica equals 12 points, which is the measurement used to define typefaces.
Pitch	Number of characters per inch.
Plotter	A type of printer that draws pictures with one or more pens based on instructions fed to it from the computer. Very useful with graphics or CAD applications.
Pointer	A symbol that appears on the screen and corresponds to the movement of the mouse or other pointing device.
Print	To generate output from the computer on to pages of paper.
Print Buffer	A portion of memory that temporarily holds the print queue.
Printer	An output device that translates signals from the computer into text and graphics on paper.
Print Head	The part of a dot-matrix printer's mechanism that contains the pins.
Print Job	An order to print certain material in a certain way at a certain time.
Print Screen	An instruction to the computer to print the screen exactly the way it is.
Print Spooler	Software that manages a print queue and lets print jobs line up one after the other.
Program	A set of instructions written in a programming language.
Prompt	A little character that appears on the screen to tell you that the program is waiting for you to enter something.
Pull-Down Menu	In a software application, a pull-down menu is a list of intriguing possibilities that appears when you select an option on the menu bar.

TASK 1D

- Open the file saved as 'Task 1C MW'.

- Insert the handwritten text at the points indicated.

- Proofread carefully and save as 'Task 1D MW'.

- Close the file.

Nicola and Simon decided to tackle *cut out*

knocking down walls

The first room was the kitchen - and they certainly had their work. "When we arrived it was in a dreadful state," says Simon. "One wall was covered in woodchip and the sink was at the wrong end of the room, so we moved it to overlook the window." Nicola felt sure there was something behind the brick arch in the kitchen but after Simon warned her not to go in case she unearthed any wires, she got the builders to do it instead. And her instincts were right - they uncovered an original bread oven and an inglenook fireplace, which now contains their Rangemaster cooker. The kitchen now has a classic farmhouse feel thanks to the colours Nicola has used.

electrical

A far cry from its original state

Monospacing	Uniform and equal spacing between the letters of words.
Mouse	A pointing device used to provide input for the computer.
Mouse Button	An area on the mouse that you press in order to make things happen. When pressed, a button makes a clicking sound. Mice have from one to three buttons, each performing different functions.
Mouse Pad	A flat surface, usually padded, used to roll your mouse around. The ball of the mouse operates best on a clean, flat surface.
Move	A command in many software products that lets you transfer objects or text from one location to another.
MS-DOS	Acronym for Microsoft Disk Operating System. The most widely used operating system for personal computers, sold also as PC-DOS by IBM.
Multimedia	Relating to video, audio, and graphics. Multimedia software combines two or more media for presentation or analysis purposes.
Nano-Second	One billionth of a second.
Near-Letter Quality	Letter-quality printing (NLQ) is produced by typewriters and daisy-wheel printers.
Network	A system of autonomous computers connected to each other for data transfer and communications. A network requires two or more computers, networking software, network adapters and cables.
New Command	A software command that produces a new document or file, as in the File New command in Microsoft Word.
Node	A single computer or terminal in a network.
Non-Volatile Memory	The memory in your computer that holds information even when you turn off your computer; read-only memory is nonvolatile, as are disk drives.
Num Lock	A key on standard PC keyboards that toggles the numeric keypad between numbers and direction keys.
Numeric Keypad	A set of keys, often adjacent to the standard keyboard keys, that include numbers and symbols for ten-key operation.
OLE	Object for object linking and embedding, an activity carried out while you are in Windows. OLE means that you can insert a document (or part of a document) created by one application inside a document created by another application, and maintain a live link between the two.
On-Line	Hooked up to a specified computer; usually said of the printer when it's connected to your PC and ready to print.
Open	To access a program or file, just as you would open a book if you wanted to read it.
Operating System	The software that controls the hardware, and which also runs your programs.
Page	The electronic unit of text that corresponds to a page in real life. The default mode is 8.5 x 11, and you can change these measurements in your word processing or page layout software.
Page Break	In word processing, the point at which one page leaves off and another begins.

TASK 1E

- Open the file saved as 'Task 1B MW'.
- Key in the following text at the end of the document as an additional paragraph.
- Insert the handwritten text.
- Proofread carefully.
- Save under a new filename, e.g. 'Task 1B with additions MW'. (Substitute your initials for 'MW' — this convention will be used throughout the book).
- Close the file.

A keen collector of [quilts, chintz, china and] old fabrics, Nicola has used them throughout to give her home a traditional look. 'I'm an avid collector of fabrics. I buy curtains, [in junkshops] particularly period florals and Fifties chintz. I love Fifties-style quilts, too. I bought [my first one] at an auction in Hampshire."

Magnetic Disk	A medium on which computer data is stored. Often called floppy disk or hard disk; a magnetic disk is a surface coated with iron oxide and magnetically charged.
Mail Merge	A process by which names and addresses (variables) are combined with a form letter 'master' to create personalised form letters. When the master form letter is printed, names and addresses from the mail merge list are inserted into key locations. Each name and address creates a new form letter from the master.
Mainframe	A powerful computer to which 'dumb' terminals are often connected. A mainframe is identified by its storage and computing capacity.
Maths Co-Processor	A separate circuit that performs floating-point arithmetic to enhance the capabilities of the CPU. Maths co-processors are available for PC computers to perform math-intensive software procedures.
MB	Abbreviation for Megabyte.
Megabyte	Approximately one million bytes. A megabyte is equal to 1,024 kilobytes, or 1,048,576 bytes.
Megahertz	One million hertz (MHz), or one million cycles per second.
Memory	Commonly refers to the chips inside a computer in which information is stored. Two types of internal memory exist: read-only memory (ROM) permanently holds information vital to the computer's operation, such as the BIOS. Random-access memory (RAM) holds information that you are currently using. The information in ROM is permanent; the information in RAM goes away when you turn off the computer.
Menu	A list of commands or options available within a program. When several options are available at a particular time, programs often present those options in menus. The menu shows each available option and, using the mouse or keyboard, you can choose a command from the menu. Such programs are often called menu-driven programs.
Menu Bar	An area, usually located at the top of the screen, that contains several menus listed across in a single line. It forms the menu bar from which you can choose commands. You choose commands by using the keyboard and the mouse.
Menu Item	An individual command or option that appears on a menu.
Message Box	A box of small windows that appears on the screen and presents a message from the program you are using.
MHz	Abbreviation for Megahertz.
Micro	A prefix that means one millionth.
Micro-Processor	The central processing chip in a microcomputer.
Micro-Second	One millionth of a second.
Microsoft	A large software company, located in Redmond, Washington, that produces MS-DOS, Windows, and a suite of best-selling application programs for the PC and Macintosh computers.
Micro-Spacing	The insertion of small spaces (smaller than one character) between words to aid in justification; used in all laser printers and some dot-matrix printers.
Milli	A prefix meaning one thousandth.
Minimise	To shrink or reduce to minimum size or capacity.
Mode	One of several distinct ways of running a program.
Monitor	Another name for a CRT screen, or terminal.
Monochrome	An adjective meaning one colour. Monochrome monitors display information in a single colour — often green or amber — on top of black.

TASK 1F

- Open the file saved as 'Task 1D MW'.

- Key in the following text at the end of the document as an additional paragraph.

- Insert the handwritten text.

- Proofread carefully.

- Save under a new filename, e.g. 'Task 1D with additions MW'.

- Close the file.

She's painted the dresser and units in National Trust Drab Green - "I love this shade of green - it gives a room a real Fifties feel" - and filled it with her chinaware. The gingham curtains complete the cottage look. *smart red*

and collection of old tins

Italic	A type style that slants text to the right for special emphasis.
Justify	To align text within the margins of a page, either left, right, centre or justified.
Keyboard	A device that looks like a typewriter and which is connected to the computer. When the user presses a key, the keyboard sends a signal to the computer, which displays the corresponding character on the screen.
Keyboard Cache	An area of memory set aside to hold a specified number of keystrokes in case you type faster than the computer's response time.
Keyboard Cover	A clear, flexible, plastic sheet that fits over a keyboard.
Keypad	A related group of keys placed together for convenience. The most common key pads are the numeric keypad and the cursor keypad.
Keys	The buttons on the keyboard.
Kilo	A prefix used in the metric system that means 1,000. So kilobyte means 1,000 bytes.
LAN	Local Area Network: a group of computers connected together to share information.
Landscape Orientation	Printing as if the page were turned sideways so that its width is longer than its height.
Laptop	A computer small enough to fit in your lap.
Laser Printer	A type of printer that uses a laser beam to generate an image and then electronically transfers it to paper.
Left-Justify	To align text flush against a left margin.
Letter Quality	Printed text that is clear enough that it looks like it came from a typewriter.
Line Editor	A program that enables you to modify one line of a text file at a time.
Linefeed	This is a signal that tells the printer to advance the page one line.
Line Number	A number used to identify lines in a document.
Line Printer	A high-speed printer that can print an entire line at once.
Link	To connect two computers together through a modem, cable or network.
List	A collection of data arranged in a certain order. Programs usually store lists as arrays or as a linked list.
List Box	A dialog box that displays a list of items. Items commonly found in a list box include filenames, printer names, directories.
Load	To transfer data from storage to memory.
Lock	To prevent access to something. Some computers have a key lock that you can use to prevent others from using your computer. Every 3.5" floppy disk has a sliding tab that can prevent the disk from being written to.
Lower Case	The opposite of capitalisation. Most text appears with the initial letter of a word in a sentence in upper case, and the rest of the text in lower case.

Unit 2

Joining Paragraphs

Creating Paragraphs

Changing Font Size

Spell Check

Paper Size

Printing

Help System	A predefined way for displaying help on the screen.
Helvetica	A common Sans Serif font that looks clean and professional. Windows and Macintosh have Helvetica as a built-in font.
Hertz	A unit of measurement for electrical vibrations, usually used in large quantities to measure the speed of a computer and abbreviated as megahertz (MHz). One hertz is equal to the number of cycles per second.
High-Capacity	Another term for high-density floppy disks.
High-Memory	On IBM compatible computers, the memory between 640K of conventional memory and 1 MB, more commonly referred to as Upper Memory.
Home Key	The key on the keyboard that usually moves the cursor to the beginning of a line or the top of a document.
Horizontal Scroll Bar	A thin strip that appears on the right side of a window, used for scrolling the contents of a window up or down.
Housekeeping	Organising (backing up and deleting) files, so that you can find them again.
Hyphenation	The ability to divide long words in half when the entire word doesn't fit in the given margin.
IBM	Acronym for International Business Machines.
Icon	A symbol that is often used in place of actual words. Many programs display icons as shortcuts to choosing commands through menus. Instead of choosing a menu command, you can just click on the icon.
Import	To load a file created by another program.
Indentation	The alignment of paragraphs within the margins of a page. Usually, the first line of every paragraph is indented several spaces to make the text easier to read.
Inkjet Printer	A type of printer that sprays ink on paper, instead of smacking an inked ribbon against the page like a dot-matrix printer does. Inkjet printers are quieter than dot-matrix printers, produce better quality printing than dot-matrix printers (but not as good as laser printers), and cost less than laser printers (but more than dot-matrix printers).
Input	Information fed into the computer for processing. Computers can receive input from a number of sources, including the keyboard, mouse or modem.
Insert Key	The key on the keyboard that has the word Insert or Ins printed on it.
Insert Mode	Programs have two modes for entering data: insert mode and overwrite mode. Insert mode means that when text is being typed, the letters that are being inserted will push the existing text forward on the screen. Most word processors have insert mode as the default mode.
Insertion Pointer	The cursor shape that shows you where letters will start appearing on the screen if you start typing on the keyboard. Some programs display the insertion pointer as a thin vertical line or as an I-shaped icon.
Install	To prepare equipment or software for use for the first time.
Interface	The connection between the computer and the person trying to use it. A keyboard is an interface and so is a monitor.
Internet	A worldwide computer network available via modem that connects universities, government laboratories, and individuals around the world. Users of the Internet can send each other electronic mail, copy files from one another, and even break into other people's computers.
Interrupt	An instruction that interrupts the computer from whatever it's doing, and makes it do something completely different.

Guidelines

1. Joining Paragraphs

Place the cursor on the first character of the second paragraph. Press the Backspace key twice — this action deletes the paragraph symbols.

2. Creating Paragraphs

Place the cursor at the point where the new paragraph is to be created and hit the Return key twice.

3. Changing Font Size

Generally, the default font size for word processing programs is 10 points. The smallest font size possible is usually 8 points and the largest font size possible is usually 72 points. Some systems provide the facility for proportional spacing to be used. With proportional spacing, the amount of space given to each character varies depending on the width of the character — see also Unit 5.

4. Spell Check

The Spell Check WP (word processing) feature puts the equivalent of a dictionary into the memory. It compares the document text to the words in the dictionary; it highlights the words in the document that don't match the spelling in the dictionary and makes possible suggestions. You have the choice of ignoring, replacing or adding the suggestion. The spelling of one word, a selection of text, or the text of an entire document can be checked. However, it is essential to proofread the document carefully even if you have checked it with a Spell Checker.

5. Paper Size

Paper comes in many sizes; the most commonly used is A4. Its orientation can be portrait or landscape. A5 paper is generally used for short documents — it is half the size of A4.

6. Printing

Use the Print command of the WP software to print the whole or part of the document.

Floppy Disk	A magnetically coated disk you use to store information for a computer. Floppy disks come in two sizes: 5.25" and 3.5". Floppy disks also come in two formats: double-density (DD) and high-density (HD).
Flush	To align text flush left or flush right.
Font	A collection of characters with predefined sizes and styles.
Font Size	The height and width of specific fonts.
Footer	A short title, word, or phrase that appears at the bottom of a page in word processors.
Foreground	When two or more windows appear on the screen, the active screen is considered to be in the foreground. Only one window may be in the foreground at one time, although any number of windows may be in the background at the same time.
Format	To prepare a floppy or hard disk for storing information for a computer.
Form Feed	To advance the paper in a printer by one sheet.
Frame	A rectangular area used by word processors for arranging text or graphics on a page.
Friction Feed	A method of moving paper by pressing rollers against the page and spinning them. Friction feed is the way typewriters advance paper a line at a time. Most inkjet and laser printers use friction feed.
Full Screen	The ability to type characters anywhere on the screen. A full-screen terminal displays information using the full screen.
Function Keys	Special keys along the top or side of a keyboard that are specifically designed for giving commands to the computer. Most computer keyboards have ten to twelve function keys, labelled F1 through F12. Function keys are shortcuts for pressing a variety of other keys.
Gigabyte	About one billion bytes, often abbreviated as GB.
GOTO	A command used to tell the computer to go to another part of the document.
Grammar Checker	A special program or built-in feature that examines a text document for grammatical errors and offers possible corrections. Most grammar checkers correct misspellings and incorrect grammar usage.
Hands-On	To teach by having the end user type on the keyboard or use the mouse of a computer.
Hard Copy	Information printed by the computer.
Hard Disk	A magnetically coated metal disk, hermetically sealed in a box and used to store massive amounts of information.
Hardware	The physical parts of a computer, printer, modem, monitor, and keyboard that you can touch.
HD	High Density 5.5" floppy disks can hold up to 1.2 MB of data. High density 3.5" floppy disks can hold up to 1.44 MB of data.
Head	The part of any floppy or hard disk drive that reads data off the spinning disk.
Header	Repetitive text (such as page number, chapter title) which appears at the top of each page in a document.
Help	Information that's supposed to show you what to do next. Help can come in the form of printed manuals or on-screen information displayed in pop-up windows.

TASK 2A

- Open the file saved as 'Task 1B with additions MW'.

- Create a new paragraph at the point beginning 'Nicola immediately set to work ... '.

- Join the paragraph commencing 'A keen collector of ... ' with the end of the previous paragraph — leave two spaces after the full stop.

- Save under a new filename 'Fabric samples'.

- Print one copy.

Keen decorators Nicola and Simon couldn't believe their luck when they first laid eyes on their Cambridgeshire home. While the back of it has a cosy, cottage-style feel to it, the facade is elegantly Georgian, and with a track record of unusual properties - the couple and their two sons previously lived in a two-storey clock tower - they fell for their new home's split personality. "As soon as we had a look round, we could see how much potential it had", says Nicola. "I have always loved doing up properties, although I have a sneaking suspicion that Simon prefers it once all the hard work is over". Nicola immediately set to work, planning new colour schemes. "I have to admit that Nicola does all the work", says Simon. "She hangs up fabric samples and looks at them for weeks before making a decision, but it always looks good in the end".

A keen collector of quilts, chintz, china and old fabrics, Nicola has used them throughout to give her home a traditional look. "I'm an avid collector of fabrics. I buy curtains in junkshops, particularly period florals and Fifties chintz. I love Fifties-style quilts, too. I bought my first one at an auction in Hampshire.

Double-Density Disk	A floppy disk that stores twice as much information in the same amount of space as a single-density disk.
Down	When a piece of computer equipment temporarily stops working.
Drag	To use the mouse for moving an object across the screen. First, you have to high light (select) the object you want by pointing to it with the mouse. Then hold down the mouse button and move the mouse. This drags the object.
Drag and Drop	To use a mouse for moving an object across the screen as a shortcut for copying or moving a group of objects.
Drive List Box	A list that displays the number of disk drives on the computer.
Drop-Down List Box	A combination of two boxes. One box lets the user type information. The second box underneath lists names that the user can choose from instead.
Edit	To modify data (e.g. text and graphics) in a file.
Elite	Typefaces that print twelve characters per inch.
End Key	The key on the keyboard with End printed on it.
Enhanced Keyboard	A keyboard that provides a numeric key pad and cursor keys separate from the main typewriter keys. Enhanced keyboards usually contain 101 keys and also are called 101-key keyboards.
Enter Key	Sometimes called the Return key; in a word processor, pressing the Enter key creates a new line.
Erase	To remove or delete.
Error Message	A cryptic note that the computer displays to let you know that the program isn't working correctly.
ESC.	Abbreviation for the Escape key. Pressing this key usually cancels whatever command you last gave the computer.
Expanded Memory	Memory used by DOS computers beyond 640K.
Extended Memory	Memory used by 80286, 386 and 486 and Pentium processors that goes beyond 1 MB.
Facing Pages	Two pages of a bound document that face each other when the document is open. Usually the even-numbered page appears on the left; the odd-numbered page appears on the right.
Fail	When something no longer works the way it's supposed to. (See also Abort, Retry, Fail, Ignore.)
Fatal Error	A problem that causes the program or computer to halt or crash completely.
Feed	To guide something into something else, usually putting paper into a printer.
Field	Space reserved for storing specific information, e.g. in mail merge.
File	Information stored on magnetic media such as a floppy or hard disk. Files can be programs, data or graphics.
File List Box	A box that lists all the files of a given directory. File list boxes are usually found in dialog boxes such as one in Windows.
File Size	The amount of disk space that a file requires for its existence, usually measured in bytes.
Fill	A command used by Drawing programs.

TASK 2B

- Open the file saved as 'Task 1D with additions MW'.
- Create a new paragraph at the point beginning 'Nicola felt sure there ... '.
- Join the paragraph commencing 'She's painted the ... ' with the end of the previous paragraph.
- Save under a new filename 'Fireplace'.
- Print one copy.

The first room Nicola and Simon decided to tackle was the kitchen - and they certainly had their work cut out. "When we arrived it was in a dreadful state," says Simon. "One wall was covered in woodchip and the sink was at the wrong end of the room, so we moved it to overlook the window." Nicola felt sure there was something behind the brick arch in the kitchen but after Simon warned her not to go knocking down walls in case she unearthed any electrical wires, she got the builders to do it instead. And her instincts were right - they uncovered an original bread oven and an inglenook fireplace, which now contains their Rangemaster cooker. A far cry from its original state, the kitchen now has a classic farmhouse feel thanks to the colours Nicola has used.

She's painted the dresser and units in National Trust Drab Green - "I love this shade of green - it gives a room a real Fifties feel" - and filled it with her chinaware and collection of old tins. The smart red gingham curtains complete the cottage look.

CPU	Central Processing Unit.
Crash	When the computer or a network suddenly stops working.
Current Directory	The directory that you are working in at any moment is the current directory and is the one from which DOS stores and retrieves files. Any directory on a hard or floppy disk can be the current directory, but only one directory can be the current directory at any given time.
Cursor	The little blinking light that appears on the screen to let you know where your next typed character will appear.
Cursor Keys	The keys on the keyboard that let you move the cursor around.
Cut	To remove text or graphics from the screen.
Cut and Paste	To remove text or graphics from the screen and make it reappear somewhere else.
Daisy Wheel	A plastic wheel on which each spoke contains a character for printing.
Default	An assumption the computer makes to perform a certain action unless the user specifies differently.
Default Directory	The directory on a hard disk that the computer uses to perform commands if it isn't given specific instruction to use a different directory.
Default Drive	The disk drive the computer looks for if it isn't given specific instructions to look anywhere else.
Del. Key	In some programs, pressing the Del. key erases the character to the left of the cursor. In other programs, pressing the Del. key erases the character to the right or the character directly beneath the cursor.
Deselect	To change your mind after selecting an item, such as by unhighlighting an item or by removing the X in an option box.
Digital	A way of representing objects using two distinct states such as On or Off, Low or High. All computers are digital computers because they consist of millions of On and Off switches.
Directory	A way of dividing a floppy or hard disk for organising files. Every disk has at least one directory called the root directory. You can create other directories and label them to keep your files that relate to different programs, data and projects separated.
Directory List Box	A display that lists directories and subdirectories in a hierarchical tree structure.
Disk	A magnetic storage device encased in a plastic case. Hard disks are encased in a box. Floppy disks may be double-density or high-density. High-density floppy disks can store two to four times as much information as double-density disks.
Disk Operating System	The main program that tells your computer how to work. Often abbreviated as DOS. On IBM and compatible computers, the disk operating system is called MS-DOS or PC-DOS.
Document	A file created by a word processor containing words or pictures.
Dot	Used to mark the decimal portion of a number. In DOS the period is used to separate a filename from its extension.
Dot Matrix	A type of printer or printout that creates letters and graphics by using lots of tiny dots. The more dots used, the sharper the image. The fewer dots used, the more the printing looks like a cheap printer.
Double-Click	To press the mouse button twice in rapid succession without moving the mouse between clicks.

TASK 2C

- Key in the text below.
- Use the Spell Check and proofread carefully.
- Save as 'Windowing MW'.
- Print one copy on A4 Paper.

Windowing Systems

A window is a rectangular area on a display screen in which text may be displayed. Several windows may be displayed on a screen at the same time. Most workstations use software that handles all screen displays by means of windows. These windowing systems normally have number features.

Windows are displayed on the screen, in a manner resembling rectangular pieces of paper placed on a desktop. Indeed one large window beneath all the others, is normally called the desktop window. Mice may be used in conjunction with windows to provide additional means for the user to interact with the system. The mouse can be made to move a pointer on the screen to an item. Mice may be used in conjunction with windows to provide additional means for the user to interact with the system. The mouse can be made to move a pointer on the screen to an item. Icons may be displayed in windows on the screen. An icon is used to represent a function. A user may move the mouse so that the pointer is over an icon and then double clicking the mouse button to 'open' the document.

The document opens with the creation of a window on the screen. Pull-down menus are special-purpose windows displayed at the top of windows, especially the desktop's.

When looking at a document in an open window, there may be a heading at the screen called 'EDIT' and if the mouse is moved above the word 'EDIT'.

Central Processing Unit	The little chip in personal computers that controls everything. Sometimes referred to as the 'brains' of the computer because it is where the basic calculating is done that translates into a file or spreadsheet.
Character	Any symbol that you can type from the keyboard.
Clip Art	Pre-drawn art that you can copy and use freely.
Clipboard	A temporary storage area used by the Macintosh, Windows and certain DOS programs for holding text or graphics. Items are automatically placed in the clipboard whenever the user chooses the CUT or COPY commands. Items remain on the clipboard until the user chooses a new item with the CUT or COPY commands. Items stored on the clipboard may be transferred to other programs.
Clock	The circuit in the computer that keeps track of the date and the time, even when the power is shut off.
Clone	A term that refers to any computer which imitates a better-known computer program. IBM, Apple and Compaq are among the better brands of computers.
Close	To remove a window from the screen. The two most common ways to close a window are to click in the window's close box with the mouse or to choose the CLOSE WINDOW command from a menu.
Close Box	The tiny little box that appears in the upper left corner of a window. Clicking the mouse cursor inside the close box removes the window from view. In most programs, the close box can be used only by a mouse.
Cold Boot	To restart equipment that has been turned off.
Colour Monitor	A computer screen that can display several colours at once. Colour monitors follow specific video graphics stands such as CGA, EGA, VGA and SVGA.
Columns	Vertical strips of text that appear on a page. Newsletters commonly display two, three, or four columns side by side. Columns are also common in spread sheets and other documents.
Computer	Any calculating device that processes data according to a series of instructions.
CONFIG.SYS	A configuration file used on MS-DOS computers that specifies the keyboard, device drivers, and amount of buffers for the computer to use.
Configure	To modify or customise a computer a certain way. Any time you add a new piece of equipment or program to your computer, you have to configure it so that it will work properly.
Constant	A value in a program that never changes.
Contiguous	When two objects are physically next to each other. Often used when describing files stored on a disk or data stored in a file.
Control Key	A special key, often abbreviated as CTRL, that works with other keys to give commands to a program.
Control Panel	A utility program that lists options for modifying hardware devices such as the mouse, keyboard and monitor.
Conventional Memory	On IBM PC and compatible computers, the first 640 kilobytes of memory (of RAM). This was the limit for a long time, and many programs still can access only conventional memory.
Co-Processor	A separate processor designed to take some of the load off the main processor to make the computer run faster.
Copy	To make an exact duplicate of an item, such as text data or files stored on a disk.
Cps	Characters per second.

TASK 2D

- Recall the file named 'Windowing MW'.
- As indicated by the proofreading symbols below:

    Insert new text
    Create and join new paragraphs.

- Use the Spell Check and proofread carefully.
- Save.
- Print one copy on A4 Paper.

Windowing Systems

or graphical images

A window is a rectangular area on a display screen in which text *or graphical images* may be displayed. Several windows may be displayed on a screen at the same time. Most workstations *and some PCs* use software that handles all screen displays by means of windows. These windowing systems normally have *a* number *of common* features.

Windows are displayed on the screen, in a manner resembling rectangular pieces of paper placed on a desktop. Indeed one large window beneath all the others, is normally called the desktop window. *NP* Mice may be used in conjunction with windows to provide additional means for the user to interact with the system. The mouse can be made to move a pointer on the screen to an item. Mice may be used in conjunction with windows to provide additional means for the user to interact with the system. The mouse can be made to move a pointer on the screen to an item. Icons may be displayed in windows on the screen. An icon is used to represent a function. *NP* A user may move the mouse so that the pointer is over an icon *which is to be selected,* and then double clicking the mouse button to 'open' the document.

RUN on The document opens with the creation of a window on the screen. *NP* Pull-down menus are special-purpose windows displayed at the top of windows, especially the desktop's.

RUN on When looking at a document in an open window, there may be a heading at the screen called 'EDIT' and if the mouse is moved above the word 'EDIT'.

A window designated as being 'on-top' obscures the view of any part of any window beneath it.

GLOSSARY

Access Time	The amount of time needed for a storage device to retrieve information.
Alignment	When used to describe text, the alignment refers to the text's relationship to the left and right margins, as in 'centred', 'left', 'justified'.
Application	Another name for a program such as a word processor, spreadsheet or database.
Arrow Keys	Special keys on the keyboard that move the cursor up, down, left or right.
* Asterisk	Used in DOS as a wildcard character. This star can represent from one to several characters, matching other filenames for use with several DOS commands.
\ Backslash	Used in MS-DOS to separate directories and filenames such as C:\WINDOWS\SYSTEM.
Backspace	The key on the keyboard that has the word Backspace printed on it. In most programs, the Backspace key erases the character to the left of the cursor.
Backup	A copy made of a file in case the original file gets destroyed. Can also refer to the actual copy of the file. In MS-DOS you use the BACKUP command to make backups of your files.
Block	Within word processing, block means a highlighted piece of text.
Boiler-Plate	A predefined document that can be used over and over again.
Bold	To display or print text more darkly.
Boot	To start up a computer.
Buffer	A storage area for holding data temporarily.
Byte	The amount of memory needed to store one character such as a letter or a number. Computer memory and disk space are measured in kilobytes, megabytes and gigabytes.
Cancel	To take back or reverse an action.
Caps Lock	The key on every computer keyboard that lets you type capital (upper-case) letters without having to press the Shift key each time. Most computers have a little light in the upper right-hand corner of the keyboard that lights up when the Caps Lock key is pressed once. If you press the Caps Lock key again, the light goes off. Unlike typewriters, pressing the Caps Lock key on a computer only produces upper-case letters.
Carriage Return	An invisible character used to end a line of text and move the cursor to the next line below; created by pressing the Enter or Return keys.
Cartridge	A self-contained removable part of a computer or printer that is usually plastic. Laser printers use toner cartridges and font cartridges.
Case	In text-formatting terms, case means the style of letters, either UPPER CASE or lower case.
Case Sensitive	The distinction made between UPPER and lower-case letters.

Unit 3

Using Overtype Mode

Deleting

TASK 19I

- Set up this varied columnar document — use appropriate scanned material (if available) or Clip Art.

- Save as 'Broken Jug'.

- Print one copy on A4 paper.

The Broken Jug
Ballina
Co Mayo
Telephone 096 72379

Proprietor Molly Maguire

Situated in the heart of Ballina this extensive pub is really warm, welcoming and cosy. Providing the very best in food and drink, their carvery lunches are superb. A haven for the tourist or the weary shopper.

The Broken Jug is also very popular with the younger age group who frequent the Night Club. The friendly and efficient staff will make your visit here truly memorable.

Golden Acres
Killala
Co Mayo
Tel: 09632183 Fax: 096 32607

Proprietors: Sean & May Golden

Situated in the historic town of Killala, this pub is a haven of relaxation and comfort. The open fire sets the tone in the old world bar, where Mayo hospitality and friendliness are always to be found.

Wholesome home cooked food is available at the bar. Close to all amenities: deep sea fishing, golf, and boat trips. You can also find evening entertainment here from Wednesdays to Sundays.

Music can be organised any night by request free of charge. The sports room is equipped for pool and darts. This is a pub that has everything. Coach tours catered for.

Lavelles Bar
Main St, Belmullet
Co Mayo

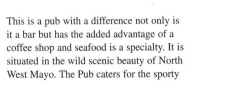

This is a pub with a difference not only is it a bar but has the added advantage of a coffee shop and seafood is a specialty. It is situated in the wild scenic beauty of North West Mayo. The Pub caters for the sporty

minded folk, a big screen is available for all those major events, and various games of skill are encouraged at the bar. Black and White award for Best Newcomer in Mayo this year.

Guidelines

1. Using Overtype Mode

Turn on Overtype mode by pressing the Insert key.
Move the cursor to the first letter of the text to be overtyped.
Key in replacement text.

Note: Turn off the Overtype mode immediately the text is edited.

2. Deleting

Letters: Incorrect or extra letters can be deleted by using either the Delete key or the Backspace key as mentioned in Unit 1.
Words: Use the command for deleting words provided by your software.
Lines: Use the command for deleting lines or parts of lines provided by your software.
Blocks (includes sentences): Use the command for deleting blocks provided by your software.

Note: Some documents in this Unit will be used again in Unit 5.

A SPORTING LIFE

In the great country house tradition, sport is everywhere at Mount Juliet.

Ride out at the Equestrian Centre. While away the hours with rod and line, along four miles of salmon-rich river. Enjoy archery and clay target shooting in quiet woodland. Play tennis or croquet. Then relax and unwind at a fully equipped spa and leisure centre. Whatever activity you choose, both equipment and professional tuition are on hand.

A ROMANTIC PROPOSAL

Dawn breaks softly across rolling green hills. In the distance, you hear the gentle clatter of hooves across a hushed Irish landscape. At gorgeous, enchanted Mount Juliet, romance finds one of its most perfect settings. Stroll along leafy paths, dine in elegant surroundings, relax by a roaring fire, then retire to a lavish guest suite, or the intimacy of your own luxury lodge. It's the start of a great love affair.

NICKLAUS' STROKE OF GENIUS

The Augusta of Europe. Mount Juliet's outstanding Jack Nicklaus Signature Golf Course has quickly earned that title. Already it has hosted the Irish Open on three occasions, winning unanimous praise from the European Tour players. While Nicklaus' layout is a stiff test for the pros, it's designed to be enjoyed by players of all standards. Superbly maintained, and playable all year round, it provides a truly exhilarating golfing experience.

DAVID LEADBETTER GOLF ACADEMY

Learn to swing like the pros at Ireland's only David Leadbetter Golf Academy. The world's most successful golf instructor offers a range of coaching programmes, tailored to *suit* players of all abilities. The Academy features a unique, Nicklaus designed 3-hole course, including pars 3, 4 and 5, and is staffed by hand-picked, Leadbetter trained coaches.

TASK 3A

- Key in the text below.
- Proofread and save as 'Fridge Freezers MW'.
- Close the file.

When you've got a growing family to look after finding a fridge freezer that's big enough to store everyone's favourite foods can be a challenge - even more so if you want one that is also inexpensive to run. With good looks and efficiency in mind Lec has designed the new Era range of streamlined fridges, freezers and fridge freezers. Most importantly, all of their Era appliances carry an energy efficiency rating A or B, so running costs are cheaper, but there are a host of other benefits, too.

Each model has deep-door storage, while toughened safety glass shelves retain the cold and make spills easy to clean. To make life really easy for you, each fridge freezer has two thermostats so the two sections are controlled separately - you can empty your fridge but leave your freezer running when you're away on holiday. So not only can you be sure you're saving yourself money throughout the year, you'll also be doing your bit to help the environment - proving that style definitely doesn't need to cost the earth.

TASK 19H

- Set up this two-page document in columnar format — use appropriate scanned material (if available) or Clip Art.

- Save as 'Mount Juliet'.

- Print one copy on A4 paper.

MOUNT JULIET
Mount Juliet
Thomastown
County Kilkenny
Ireland

DAILY RATES & ACCOMMODATION

Deep amid the rolling green hills of Ireland's beautiful south east, lies Mount Juliet, a 1500 acre sporting paradise, rich in history and tradition. Nothing can prepare you for the warmth of its welcome, or the depth of its peace, as carefully preserved as the estate's magnificently luxurious 18th-century mansion. Enjoy golf, horse riding, fishing, shooting, tennis, and a fully equipped spa and leisure centre. Or simply relax in the most idyllic surroundings imaginable.

MIDWEEK BREAK

Escape to the unhurried elegance of Ireland's great Country Estate, and prepare to be spoiled on a grand scale. Choose from a variety of luxurious accommodation, sample exquisite cuisine, be part of the estate's rich sporting life, unwind at one of its cosy, welcoming bars. For two unforgettable nights, watch the world and its cares disappear, as Mount Juliet casts its irresistible spell. Your only thought will be of a return visit.

TASK 3B

- Open the file named 'Fridge Freezers MW'.
- Delete single letters with either the Backspace key or Delete key.
- Delete words with the relevant WP command.
- Make other editing changes, as necessary.
- Use the Spell Check and proofread carefully.
- Save as 'Freezers MW'.
- Close the file.

(large)

When you've got a growing family to look after finding a fridge freezer that's
big enough to store everyone's ~~favourite~~ foods can be a challenge - even more *del*
so if you want one that is ~~also~~ inexpensive to run. With good looks and *del*
efficiency in mind Lec has designed the new ~~Era~~ range of streamlined fridges, *del*
freezers and fridge freezers. ~~Most importantly,~~ all of their Era appliances carry *del* UC
an energy efficiency rating A or B, so running costs are cheaper, but there are
~~a host of~~ other benefits, too. *del*

del Each model has deep-door storage, while toughened safety glass shelves
retain the cold ~~and make spills easy to clean.~~ [To make life really easy for you, NP
each fridge freezer has two thermostats so the two sections are controlled
separately - you can empty your fridge but leave your freezer running when
you're away on holiday. So not only can you be sure you're saving yourself
money throughout the year, you'll also be ~~doing your bit to~~ help the (ing)
environment - proving that style definitely doesn't need to cost ~~the earth~~. a lot.

The Sign Post – Newsheet of the Week

Junior AUL

The AUL Juniors were crowned Division 3 champions last week and the U-12s by virtue of their two wins and a draw, won the Premier League title.

Lickeen Hall AFC

In this, the final Newsletter of the summer, we can happily report the clinching of the 2 League trophies to go with the President's Cup Victory.

Lickeen Athletic Club

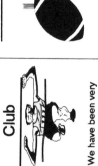

We have been very busy competing at the County and Leinster Championships in recent weeks.

Tennis

Three cheers for our Munster Branch players: Teresa White, Paul Strong, Michelle Deasy and John Curtin.

College Corinthians

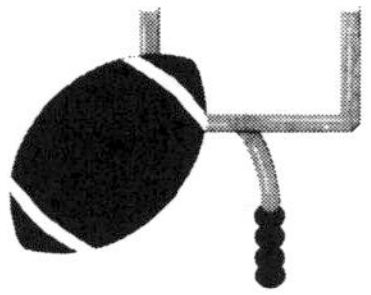

Following their tremendous start to the season, Corinthian Boys under twelve team travelled to Currakeen midweek to play Currakeen Ltd hoping of another victory. Unfortunately, it was not to be.

Soccer

Soccer accolade of the week goes to the worthy winner: Paudie Roche.

Newsflash World Cup Giveaway!

Purchase a 6-pack of Coke/Sprite or Fanta and get a FREE LIMITED EDITION World Cup Glass. Available while Stocks last!

Flowers

See the chrysanthem-ums growing. Thousands of show blooms and sprays from last week of July to Christmas.

PHONE CHRIS AT: 870654 UP TO 6 PM DAILY

Less than a mile from Lickeen on right by roundabout

Greetings

THE SIGN POST EDITORIAL TEAM WISHES EVERYBODY A VERY HAPPY HOLIDAY SEASON.

The Flagship Station of the South

Newsflash! Annual Parish Barbecue: June 30th   Page 7

[Handwritten annotations: "brush script (28)", "Century gothic (18)", "Hold (14)", "Algeria (iv)", "brush script (17)"]

TASK 3C

- Key in the text below.
- Proofread and save as 'Notting Hill MW'.
- Close the file.

Working in such a flamboyant industry, you might expect Charles Worthington's home to be a riot of colour, but you couldn't be further from the truth. Twice voted British Hairdresser of the Year (1996 and 1998), Charles travels extensively promoting his Charles Worthington Hair & Beauty company, and its range of best-selling products. Add to this regular TV appearances, a group of London salons to run and a client list that includes Ulrika Jonsson, and you can understand why he treasures every second that he gets to spend at home, which for him is a Georgian house on a tree-lined street in London's Notting Hill. "I love being at home. When I'm in London I like to spend as much time as I can here, so it's vital that it's really comfortable."

Charles, has created the ultimate in relaxed living with a cool palette of whites and creams, stripped floorboards and bleached furniture. This was the very first house he saw when he started house hunting in the area nearly four years ago and as soon as he saw it Charles knew his search for the perfect home was over. The house has many original features, including very tall windows, many of which Charles has been able to leave bare because the house isn't overlooked, allowing lots of natural light to flood in.

TASK 19G

- Set up this two-page, six-column document on A4 landscape paper.
- Save as 'Sign Post'.
- Print one copy on A4 paper.

The Sign Post
Lickeen Parish Newsletter

The Sign Post ~ Brush Script (30)
Lickeen Parish Newsletter ~ Footlight MT Light (20)

Thirteenth Sunday in Ordinary Time — *Bookman Old Style (10)*

6 June 1994

Ole. Ole Ole Ole, Ole, Ole

****

Saturday night - Lickeen was almost a ghost-town. All those interested were glued to their television sets to see how Ireland would fare in their opening clash with Italy. We sat there, rivetted, probably kicking the table in front of us, knowing how every ball should be kicked and raising lumps on our heads as we knew how each high cross should be met. Indeed, if we had been playing the result would have been a lot more comfortable than the one-goal margin. In the end, we all ended up euphoric. People were out in the streets giving vent to their joy. I suppose the thought must have crossed many minds that, while it was great to enjoy the celebrations how much better it would have been to have actually been at Giants Stadium at the event itself

Brush Script (16)

Baptisms

We welcome into our Christian family:

Joseph Nigel Lynch, 5 Manor Lawn. Jane Nora Cotter, 23 Upper Manor View.

Weddings

Congratulations to Tom Greene of 23 Upper Rochestown View. Cork. and Patricia O'Sullivan of "St Alban's", Cork Road. Fermoy, Co Cork, on their recent wedding.

In Sympathy

We extend our deepest sympathy to Larry Clancy of Russell Drive on the recent death of his father-in-law, John O'Sullivan, of Donnybrook.

Money Matters

Offertory Collections between St Patrick's and St Peter's Churches last week-end amounted to £2,345.

Golf Diary

The main event in the past week was surely the Lady Captain's (Matilda Daly's) prize stories. Rita Lynch brought in a magnificient card again.

Academic

Congratulations to Edward Roche. 23 Lickeen View on being conferred. He is a credit to his proud parents and an example to his classmates.

Newsflash! Annual Parish Barbecue: June 30th

Page 6

Arial Narrow ((6)

Celtic
Gothic ((8)

TASK 3D

- Open the file named 'Notting Hill MW'.

- Delete single letters with either the Backspace key or Delete key.

- Delete words/lines/blocks with the relevant WP command.

- Make other editing changes, as necessary.

- Use the Spell Check and proofread carefully.

- Save as 'Relaxed Living MW'.

---

del ~~Working in such a flamboyant industry~~, you might expect Charles *UC*
Worthington's home to be a riot of colour, but you couldn't be further from the
truth. Twice voted British Hairdresser of the Year (~~1996 and 1998~~), Charles *del*
travels extensively promoting his ~~Charles Worthington~~ Hair & Beauty *del*
company, and its range of best-selling products. Add to this regular TV
appearances, a group of London salons to run and a client list ~~that includes~~ *del*
~~Ulrika Jonsson~~, and you can understand why he treasures every second that
he gets to spend at home, which for him is a Georgian house on a tree-lined
street in London's Notting Hill. ["I love being at home. When I'm in London I *NP*
like to spend as much time as I can here, so it's vital that it's really comfortable.

NP Charles, has created the ultimate in relaxed living with a cool palette of whites
and creams, stripped floorboards and bleached furniture. This was the very
first house he saw when he started house hunting in the area nearly four years
ago, and as soon as he saw it Charles knew his search for the perfect home
was over. [The house has many ~~original~~ features, including very tall windows, *del*
many of which Charles has been able to leave bare because the house isn't
⊙ overlooked, ~~allowing lots of natural light to flood in~~. *del*

TASK 19F

- Set up this document on A4 portrait paper in a two-column format — use a variety of font types and sizes.
- Save as 'Isle of Wight'.
- Print one copy on A4 paper.

THE BEAUTIFUL ISLE OF WIGHT!

Captain's Cabin
(Eat by the Sea's Edge)

Courier (20)

Colwell Bay
Early Breakfast 7.30: Sat 8.30 Sun - Fri

OPEN TILL LATE
Easter till October

- *Morning Coffee Teas Sandwiches Snacks*
- *Ploughman's & Salads Home Cooked Meals*

HOT & COLD MEALS SERVED ALL DAY
Lake, Train Station is close by and the famous cliff path walk

We are also on the main bus routes
NO SUPPLEMENTS * NO RESTRICITONS *
- OPEN ALLYEAR -

Shadow + arjin (14)

A REALLY PRETTY LITTLE PLACE

script (16)

LICENSED RESTAURANT

Chargrills
exican* Fresh Pizza

Cocktails etc
Children Welcome
PARTY BOOKINGS

Arial Narrow (10)

Eating Out
When you are away from home you can enjoy to the full the delights and pleasures of eating out. The Isle of Wight has more than 100 restaurants and cafes to choose from, and here are some suggestions for eating on the island.

The range is very wide. From restaurants offering top cuisine to small places offering traditional cream teas. When you go in search of food, don't ignore the pubs. Many serve food of a very high standard. The Island being surrounded by sea is noted particularly for its sea food. Many restaurants and pubs offer fish dishes based on the days catch of lobster crab and shell fish and you will not find better in the United Kingdom. Footlight MT (14)

You should also try the islands own wines produced at the local vineyards at Barton Manor by Rosemary and Morton Manor.

K E A T S
Green
H O T E L
script (18)

4 King's Road
Shanklin
Isle of Wight

Tel. (0983) 87987

KARD TIMES CAFE
OPEN EVERY DAY
(6.30 - 11.00)
(Last Orders: 10.30)

The Hideway
Open Daily

Morning Coffee Lunches
Afternoon Teas
Evening Meals

- **Reasonable Prices**
- **Large Beer and Tea Garden**

(T Shadow   Arial Narrow (18)

FOOD - GLORIOUS FOOD!

TASK 3E

- Key in the text below.
- Use the Spell Check and proofread carefully.
- Save as 'Bathrooms MW'.
- Close the file.

You might not think that a humble radiator could evoke fond childhood memories but when Sue Whitney found one that reminded her of the bathroom in her grandparent's farmhouse she decided to go all out to create her own rustic-style retreat. Having splashed out on the radiator of a new central heating system, Sue, who lives with her husband Roy and 12-year-old daughter, Anna, had to come up with inventive ideas for the rest of the scheme. "The bathroom is a bit nondescript and very tired looking - I'd love to freshen it up.", said Sue. This is where House Beautiful style experts, Debbie and Jessica came in. As the existing bathroom suite was only five years old, Sue didn't really want to replace it, so Debbie suggested simply giving it a fresh new look. The bathroom is big enough and all the features that Sue needs to create a country-style look are already in place.

The wooden panelling and pretty blue colour scheme are a good starting point for a rustic makeover. Although Jessica and Debbie both liked the existing floral-patterned blind they decided to replace it with a red-and-white gingham fabric that would fit in with the bathroom's new look as well as matching the existing border tiles and blue walls.

TASK 19E

- Set up this document on A4 portrait paper in a two-column format — illustrate using WordArt, Clip Art, Lines etc.

- Save as 'Tropics'.

- Print one copy on A4 paper.

Banish your flying blues!

BORU TRAVEL TEAM CAN OFFER YOU:
arial -rounded MT (18)

Sandy Beaches

Sailing in the Tropics

Spectacular Views

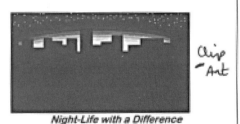
Night-Life with a Difference

clip Art

You've tried the rest... now try the Best!

AMAZING VALUE!
October Bank-Holiday Breaks

Paris by sea from	£100
Paris via UK from	£190
Rhineland via UK from £110	
Valkenburg via UK from 181	

shading

- Cheapest air tours to Italy, Germany, France and the low Countries.
- All European destinations catered for:

FREE INSPECTION TOUR
By air to ITALY

VISITING:

- Florence
- Venice
- San Marino

The No. 1 Inspection Tour for Business Persons.

BORU TRAVEL COMPANY
Crescent House
14 Gilabbey St
Dublin 2.
Tel: 01-667 8989
Fax: 01-668 4772

BORU
TRAVEL

- Drawing

Think Boru for Value

TASK 3F

- Open the file named 'Bathrooms MW'.
- Delete single letters with either the Backspace key or Delete key.
- Delete words/lines/blocks with the relevant WP command.
- Make other editing changes, as necessary.
- Use the Spell Check and proofread carefully.
- Save as 'Floral Blinds MW'.
- Close the file.

You might not think that a ~~humble~~ radiator could evoke fond childhood memo- *del*
ries but when Sue Whitney found one that reminded her of the bathroom in
del
del
del
her grandparent's ~~farm~~house she decided to go all out to create her own
~~rustic-style~~ retreat. ~~Having splashed out on the radiator of a new central~~ *del*
~~heating system~~, Sue, who lives with her husband Roy and 12-year-old
daughter, Anna, had to come up with inventive ideas for the rest of the
scheme. "The bathroom is a bit nondescript and very tired looking - I'd love
to freshen it up.", said Sue. This is where ~~House Beautiful~~ style experts, *del*
Debbie and Jessica came in. As the existing bathroom suite was only five
years old, Sue didn't really want to replace it, so Debbie suggested simply
giving it a fresh new look. [The bathroom is big enough and all the features *NP*
that Sue needs to create a country-style look are already in place.

The wooden panelling and pretty blue colour scheme are a good starting point
for a rustic makeover. Although Jessica and Debbie both liked the existing
floral-patterned blind they decided to replace it with a ~~red-and-white~~ (green) gingham
fabric that would fit in with the bathroom's new look as well as matching the
~~existing border tiles and~~ blue walls. *del*

TASK 19D

- Set up this document on A4 portrait paper in a three-column format — illustrate using WordArt, Clip Art, Lines etc.

- Save as 'Jumbo'.

- Print one copy on A4 paper.

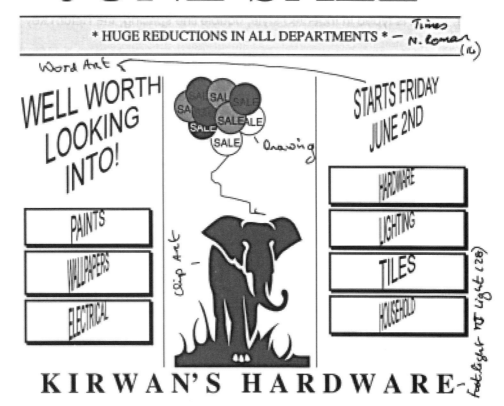

Unit 4

Margins

Moving a Block

Copying a Block

Line Spacing

AT LEISURE IN THE COUNTRYSIDE

A (partial (16)

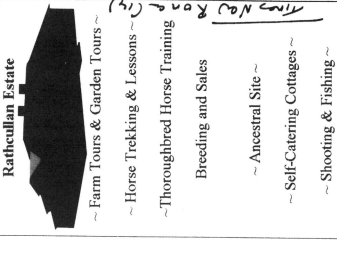

Rathcullan Estate

Timing Not Kerve (12)

~ Farm Tours & Garden Tours ~

~ Horse Trekking & Lessons ~

~ Thoroughbred Horse Training

Breeding and Sales

~ Ancestral Site ~

~ Self-Catering Cottages ~

~ Shooting & Fishing ~

~ Golf Course ~

For further information, without obligation, on any of our activities please contact:-

Rathcullan Estate Office
Rathcullan.
Tel. 009 89765 Fax: 980765

Rathcullan Golf Course

This outstanding championship six hole developments was opened to the golfing public in May 1982. The par 69 course provides the golfer with the most challenging golf to be found in Kilgubban The River Fiora comes into play on four of the holes with the course landscaped around the breathtaking Rathcullan Gardens. The course is built to the highest specifications with sand based greens and tees. In keeping with the Wonderland theme of the course the golfer has to raft across the river between the fourth fairway and green

Open to Green Fees 7 days a week

Location

Rathcullan is on the main Kilmok-Foxrock Road (Signposted)

	Miles	Km
To Kilmock	30	48
To Foxrock	190	304
To Rockrow	159	254
To Millwall	2	3

Professional Available by Arrangement

Accommodation

Self-catering accommodation is available on the Estate for rental. the bungalows are situated close to all State activities and enjoy beautiful peaceful surroundings. A lively night life maybe e found in the local towns and villages. each bungalow can accommodate 4 people and all have electric central heating and water heating facilities. Bed linen provided.

Gardens

The gardens in the Victorianstyle take advantage of the natural features and contours provided by the valley land the Fiora River running though it. The spectacular Rock Gardens and Azalea Gardens contain a variety of unusual plants.

Farm

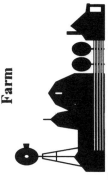

The Rathcullan farm is a model farm featuring state of the art machineryOpen to the public for groups and organised tours by appointment.

Guidelines

1. Margins

Default margins: Software has many default settings (see Glossary) including default margins — the default settings apply, unless set otherwise.

Setting margins: Margins can be changed from the pre-set default margins to a margin setting of your choice.

2. Moving a Block (also known as 'Cut and Paste')

Highlight the block to be moved.
Use the command to move (or cut) the block from its original position.
Move the cursor to the new location of the block.
Use the Paste command to relocate the block.

3. Copying a Block

Highlight the block to be copied.
Use the command to copy the block.
Move the cursor to the location for the copied block.
Use the Paste command to copy the block to the screen.

Note: Cutting literally removes the data from its original position whereas **copying** leaves the original as it is.

4. Line Spacing

Single-line Spacing: Word processing software is pre-set to single-line spacing, i.e. the text is typed one line after the other, without a clear line in between. The Return key must be hit twice between paragraphs when the text is typed in single-line spacing.

Double-line Spacing: The text is typed one line after the other, with a clear line in between. The Return key must be hit twice between paragraphs when blocked text is typed in double-line spacing. This is necessary to distinguish one paragraph from the other. (If text is typed in indented style, double-line spacing, the Return key is only hit once.)

1.5 Line Spacing: The text is typed one-and-one-half times that of single-line spacing. For example, if 10-point text is spaced at 1.5 lines, the line spacing is approximately 15 points.

Note: The documents in this Unit will be used again in Unit 5.

TASK 19C

- Set up this two-page document on A4 landscape paper — illustrate using Clip Art, Lines etc.

- Save as 'Leisure'.

- Print one copy on A4 paper.

At Leisure in the Countryside

Riding School

Come & enjoy the most beautiful Trekking throughout the unspoilt farmlands and woods of Kilgubban. At Rathcullan Estate, treks from one hour, to as long as you like, are available.

For those not keen to ride, enjoy the 'jarvey experience' in a traditional horse & trap along the lands of Rathcullan. The Rathcullan Horse Centre can offer you the opportunity to learn to ride to the highest standard.

Using our farmlands we have developed an all weather cross country course, dressage and showjumping arenas and an all-weather riding arena.

Commercial gallop available on request: five furlong straight and a mile circuit.

Schooling hurdles and fences are also a feature at the Horse Centre.

Race Horses

Rathcullan Estate has a good selection of both Flat and National Hunt Race Horses in training. They race in the blue and white colours of The Rathcullan Horse Centre Limited and the now familiar blue and gold racing silks of Rathcullan Farms Limited. The horses are in training in Ireland, Germany and America and are racing with great success. Rathcullan Estate has also a good selection of brood mares and their progeny will be the backbone to the future. Rathcullan Estate would be happy to train and buy horses for a prospective owner.

Rathcullan

The Sweeney Ancestral Site is located on the Estate property at Kilquane. In the near future it is planned to rebuild the Rathcullan Cottage to its original specification. A Museum and Art gallery are also planned for which a 1911 Model T Ford and 1955 Ford Consul have already been bought. Escorted visits to the ruins are available by appointment.

Shooting

Fully keepered shoots from 1st September to 31st January. We rear and release our own high quality Duck and Pheasant. Our shoot is set in 120 acres of beautiful woodland with Flight Ponds and Snipe Bog. We provide shooting for all enthusiasts:- Duck and Snipe shooting from 1st September to 31st January. Pheasant and Woodcock shooting from 1st November to 31st January and Rabbit and Pigeon shooting all year round. Highest safety standards are strictly enforced.

Fishing

Fish private waters on the best stretches of the River Fiora. Relax in the Tranquil setting of the Estate grounds with one mile of double bank and one mile of single bank fishing in beautiful Kilgubban. Fish for Salmon or Sea Trout and test your skill against our finest quarry.

TASK 4A

- Key in the text below; use default margins and single-line spacing.

- Use the Spell Check and proofread carefully.

- Save as 'Strawberry Pink MW'.

- Print one copy, if time permits.

- Close the file.

Louise Green is the last person you could accuse of being stuck in a decorating rut. A career in fashion means she's always up-to-date with the latest trends and this goes for her home, as well as her wardrobe. Furniture, colour schemes and soft furnishings are all changed regularly. "After a while I get bored and can't wait to update the look of a room", says Louise. "Some people might see it as an obsession, but I think it's quite natural. You wouldn't want to wear the same dress year in year out, so why should you always live with the same coloured walls."

She's not afraid to experiment with colour. Safe, timeless neutrals are definitely out - as the brilliant shades in the kitchen goes to show. Louise has redecorated the walls in this room more than four times in the last ten years. First, she painted them neutral, then she tried rose. Next she covered them with a plaster effect and now they are vibrant with hot colours, including orange, lime and strawberry pink. "We looked at the colour chart and went straight for the fruit shades", she explains. "I've managed to leave the original limed oak finish alone, but the walls have made the whole room much more contemporary."

The mix of rustic furniture and sunny colours gives this room a strong Mexican flavour - echoed by the striking tiled table, wrought iron chairs and Gothic-style light fitting.

TASK 19B

- Set up the document below — use the Drawing tools of Word to help recreate this example.

- Save as 'Eurostat'.

- Print one copy on A4 paper.

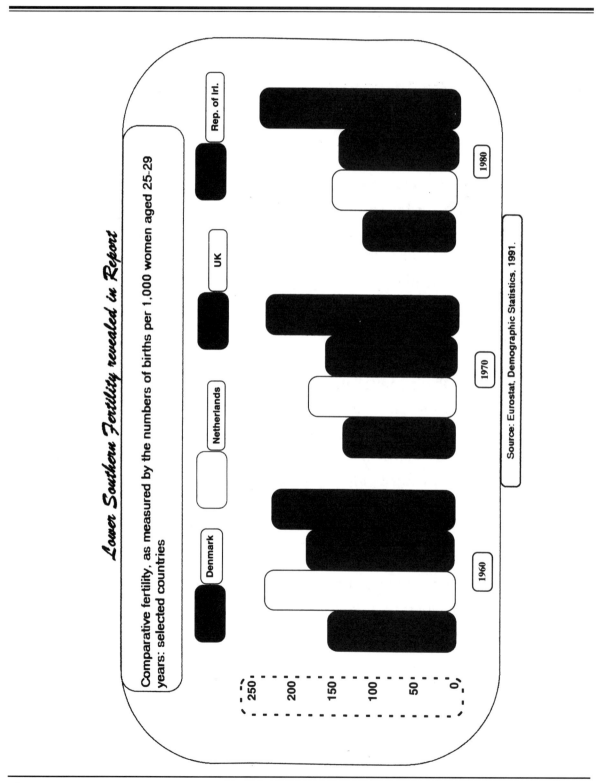

TASK 4B

- Open the file named 'Strawberry Pink MW'.

- Change both the left and right margins to 1".

- Move text, as indicated.

- Make suggested editing changes.

- Make a new page break at the end of the document.

- Make a copy of the document and paste onto the new page.

- Use the Spell Check and proofread carefully.

- Save as 'Rustic Furniture MW'.

- Close the file.

---

change 'c' of 'colour' to 'Colour'

Louise Green is the last person you could accuse of being stuck in a decorating rut. A career in fashion means she's always up-to-date with the latest trends and this goes for her home, as well as her wardrobe. Furniture, colour *move* schemes and soft furnishings are all changed regularly. "After a while I get bored and can't wait to update the look of a room", says Louise. "Some people might see it as an obsession, but I think it's quite natural. You wouldn't want to wear the same dress year in year out, so why should you always live with the same coloured walls".

del

move She's not afraid to experiment with colour. ~~Safe~~, timeless neutrals are definite- *uc* ly out - as the brilliant shades in the kitchen goes to show. Louise has redecorated the walls in this room more than four times in the last ten years. First, she painted them neutral, then she tried rose. Next she covered them with a plaster effect and now they are a vibrant of hot colours, including *move* orange, lime and strawberry pink. "We looked at the colour chart and went straight for the fruit shades", she explains. "I've managed to leave the original limed oak finish alone, but the walls have made the whole room much more contemporary."

The mix of rustic furniture and sunny colours gives this room a strong Mexican flavour - echoed by the striking tiled table, wrought iron chairs and Gothic-style light fitting.

TASK 19A

- Set up the document below — use the Drawing tools of Word to help recreate this example.

- Save as 'Epson'.

- Print one copy on A4 paper.

THE EPSON - PRINTER OF THE 90's

HOW TO ENTER THE 21st CENTURY SUPEREDRAW FORYOUR EPSON STYLUS 500 INJET PRINTER

Drawing

POST OR FAX TODAY

Simply fill in all the details below and post or fax your entry to:

SuperDraw of the 21st Century
456a Upper Mount St Dublin 2 Tel. 01 23465 Fax. 56783

— Italics

ENTRY FORM

Company (Block Capitals)_____

Name _____ Position_____

Address _____

Tel No. _____ Fax No_____

1. Do you use a PC?   ☐ Yes   ☐ No
    If so, state make and model.
    _____

2. Date of Purchase (approx.) _____

3. Do you intend changing your PC?   ☐ Yes   ☐ No
    If Yes please circle: 3mths   6mths   12mths

4. Do you intend upgrading your PC?   ☐ Yes   ☐ No
    If Yes, please circle: 3mths   6mths   12mths

5. Do you intend changing your printer?   ☐ Yes   ☐ No

6. Would you like to receive a catalogue free of charge? ☐ Yes   ☐ No

Signed _____   *Date* _____

TASK 4C

- Key in the text below; use default margins and single-line spacing.

- Use the Spell Check and proofread carefully.

- Save as 'Secluded Garden MW'.

- Print one copy, if time permits.

- Close the file.

The result is a secluded spot that Ashley and Susie are only too happy to put to good use, entertaining family and friends here throughout the summer. In fact, this area is a makeshift leisure centre in more ways than one.

Despite the unusual mix of shrubs in this area, it's been designed so it doesn't need much maintenance. "The plants seem to do their own thing down here - we just clip them back now and again", says Susie. "I love sitting down here. Nobody can see me from the house and it's so peaceful."

Ashley has arranged the seating to catch the sun at different times of the day. "I love to sit on the patio - you can see all the way down the garden from here - it's wonderful." And with a low-maintenance garden that has colour and interest all year round, there's plenty of time for Susie and him to soak up the scenery.

Guidelines

A variety of documents can be created in Word using features such as:

1. **WordArt**

2. **Clip Art**

3. **Drawing Tools**

4. **Frames**

5. **Shading**

6. **Shadows**

TASK 4D

- Open the file named 'Secluded Garden MW'.

- Change the line spacing to double-line spacing.

- Change both the left and right margins to 1". ✓

- Move text, as indicated.

- Make suggested editing changes.

- Make a new page break at the end of the document.

- Make a copy of the document and paste onto the new page.

- Use the Spell Check and proofread carefully.

- Save as 'Rustic Furniture MW'.

- Close the file.

The result is a secluded spot that Ashley and Susie are only too happy to put to good use, entertaining family and friends here throughout the summer. In *trs* fact, this area is a makeshift leisure centre in more ways than one.

Move Despite the unusual mix of shrubs in this area, it's been designed so it doesn't need much maintenance. "The plants seem to do their own thing down here - we just clip them back now and again", says Susie. "I love sitting down here. Nobody can see me from the house and it's so peaceful."

Ashley has arranged the seating to catch the sun at different times of the day. "I love to sit on the patio - you can see all the way down the garden from here - it's wonderful." And with a low-maintenance garden that has colour and *uc* interest all year round, there's plenty of time for Susie and him to soak up the *del* scenery.

Unit 19

WordArt

Clip Art

Drawing Tools

Frames

Shading

Shadows

TASK 4E

- Key in the text below; use default margins.

- Use the Spell Check and proofread carefully.

- Save as 'Stainless Steel MW'.

- Print one copy, if time permits.

- Close the file.

Most head chefs are used to being rushed off their feet, but Stewart Wall has really got his hands full at the moment. The restaurant's owners, actress Amy Ash and her husband Julian Lee are branching out, and when a second restaurant opens in Leeds, Stewart will be commuting between the two. "I'm looking forward to it actually. I'm terribly lucky seeing as I only got into cooking with a push from my brother - but he retired from the business after he won the pools!'

When Stewart does get a chance to relax, though, you're most likely to find him at home in his own kitchen, cooking for his French partner, Cecilia. "She's keeping me almost as busy as I am at work!", he said.

His home kitchen looks just as professional as his working one. To create an efficient workspace, Stewart has gone for a selection of smart, low-level stainless-steel units, a huge cooker and granite work surfaces and floor. It's a far cry from the number of run-down seventies units that the couple discovered when they first moved into their East London flat.

DP or WP?

Communication problems

1. To some extent, communication problems are built into a centralised WP operation. In a regular working relationship, typists learn to handle individual authors differently. Some tolerate editing, others don't. Terminology and handwriting become familiar. More importantly, authors can communicate their needs directly. Filling out forms and following complex procedures to get a letter typed is not necessarily good use of an author's time.

2. In the rush to set up WP centres, the inherent value of author-typist communication has been overlooked. The very nature of the centre deliberately restricts author-typist communication. Usually, authors are not allowed contact with anyone except the supervisor.

Responsiveness

*   Responsiveness is often a matter of perception. Related problems, such as slow turnaround time, can occur whether typing is centralised or not. However, the frustration is easier to deal with locally. The reasons for delay there are apparent, whereas in the centre, it is usually cause for feeling ignored.

*   There are some other, more subtle ways in which centres are unresponsive. For example, centres tend to impose a uniform standard of typing on the entire organisation. This inhibits special requests even though the standard format may not be suitable in all cases, and stifles any feeling of creativity for the typists.

Page 12

TASK 4F

- Open the file named 'Stainless Steel MW'.

- Change the line spacing of the first paragraph to 1.5.

- Change the line spacing of the second paragraph to double-line spacing.

- Change both the left and right margins to 3 cm.

- Move text, as indicated.

- Make suggested editing changes.

- Make a new page break at the end of the document.

- Make a copy of the document and paste onto the new page.

- Use the Spell Check and proofread carefully.

- Save as 'Restaurant MW'.

- Close the file.

---

del ⊙ Most head chefs are used to being rushed off their feet, but Stewart Wall has really got his hands full at the moment. The restaurant's owners, actress Amy Ash and her husband Julian Lee, are branching out, and when a second restaurant opens in Leeds, Stewart will be commuting between the two. "I'm *del* looking forward to it actually. I'm terribly lucky seeing as I only got into cooking with a push from my brother - but he retired from the business after he *del* won the pools!'

Move

lc When Stewart does get a chance to relax, though, you're most likely to find *UC del* him at home in his own kitchen, cooking for his French wife, Cecilia. "She's *del* keeping me almost as busy as I am at work!", he said.

His home kitchen looks just as professional as his working one. To create an *NP* efficient workspace, Stewart has gone for a selection of smart, low-level stainless-steel units, a huge cooker and granite work surfaces and floor. It's a far cry from the number of run-down seventies units that the couple discovered when they first moved into their East London flat.

TASK 18G

- Set up this two-page document as displayed; use paragraph numbering, bullets and headers and footers.

- Save as 'Control'.

- Print one copy on A4 portrait paper.

Header: DP or WP?

The politics of centralised word processing   Helv (16)

- What does all this have to do with WP? First of all, whether you centralised DP or WP, you are likely to run into the same set of problems. These same four problems can be critical when something as valuable as WP is at issue.

Control

- If DP is information, WP is communications - an equally important resource. It is every manger's link with the rest of the world: top management, employees, customers. No one willingly gives us control over communications.

Priority Conflicts — Script (26)

Priority conflicts are always difficult to manage. Let's look at a specific case. A

large engineering organisation sets up a WP centre. Dictation equipment

is installed. Encouraging use of dictation is the centre manager's top

priority. A policy of processing all dictation work first is established.

When the chairman finds out, he hits the ceiling.

The company's priorities are engineering projects. Designer's work comes first

regardless of how it arrives. Yet even within that established priority,

there are still difficult conflicts that must be resolved.

Continued Overleaf

Unit 5

Fonts

Ruler Line

Status Bar

Line Spacing

Main Headings

Indenting the First Line of a Paragraph

Alignment of Text

Bold

Italics

Underlining

Search and Replace

HEADER: DEFINING YOUR WORKLOAD II

- Consultants
  Advantages. Knows WP especially if you find a good one knows other organisations. Can save you from reinventing others' mistakes. Has a tested study methodology.
  Disadvantages. Expensive. Has to learn your organisation.
  Comments. Look for someone who will work with your staff, who will develop in-house skills. Obtain a specific written proposal and check references carefully. A good consultant will be willing to support your in-house team as an expert resource.

- Suppliers
  Advantages. No cost. Often quite knowledgeable in the field.
  Disadvantages. Obvious biases. Can create a sense of obligation even if not deliberate.
  Comments. Ask the supplier to share collected data with you, not just conclusions. Be wary of suppliers who use "industry standards" to decide on the right number of machines. The industry tends to be theirs, not yours.

- Develop a work plan
  First define your scope of investigation. Don't bite off too much at once, two or three smaller studies are easier to manage than one large one.

FOOTER: MODERNISE OR NOT TODAY!

Guidelines

1. Fonts

Font Type/Font Size are a collection of characters with predefined sizes and styles. All modern software has a default font type and font size but the user can choose from a variety of different fonts and font sizes.

2. Ruler Line

The Ruler Line is a strip at the top marked in units of measurement, such as inches but the option is there to set to measurements other than inches. WP software provides the option to display or hide the Ruler.

3. Status Bar

The Status Bar, which is a horizontal area at the bottom of the document window in Microsoft Word, provides information about the current state of what you are viewing in the window.

4. Main Headings

These may be blocked at the left-hand margin or centred on the typing line. They are usually typed in CLOSED capitals or S P A C E D capitals. If the heading is typed in lower case with initial capitals, it should be underlined. Allow two line spaces after the main heading at the beginning of an exercise.

5. Indenting the First Line of a Paragraph (Tabs – see Unit 6)

Default Tab stops are pre-set at .5" intervals on the **Ruler Line**.
A **button** on the keyboard, marked with forward and backward arrows, known as the **Tab key** can be depressed to move the cursor to the pre-set tabs.
Pressing the Tab key once and then typing in text will create what is known as **Indented Paragraphs** — the following block can be termed as such:

> John and Rita couldn't believe their luck when they first laid eyes on their Limerick home. The back of it has a cosy, cottage-style feel to it.

Note: WP software also includes a Menu command for indenting the first line of a paragraph.

TASK 18F

- Set up the following two-page document as displayed; use paragraph numbering and headers and footers.
- Save as 'Objectives'.
- Print one copy on A4 portrait paper.

HEADER: DEFINING YOUR WORKLOAD II

The preliminary steps outlined below will smooth the way.

1. Define objectives

   Decide in advance what benefits you expect or will accept. Be very wary of committing yourself to cash savings as the sole criterion for justifying the cost of your new system. You may find at the conclusion that there is a valid case for WP in your company. You may be able solve many of the problems you talked about in the earlier text but you may find that doing so will cost you some money. Think of your objectives through carefully, and then stick to them.

2. Obtain management support:

   No doubt you have heard that before, but it's important. Make sure management understands and is committed to the same objectives. Otherwise at the end they may reject any proposal that doesn't cut secretarial staffing.

   Assemble the survey team

   You basically have three choices: an in-house team, consultants or suppliers. Their relative merits are these:

   - In-house study team

     Advantages. Knows the organisation. Builds commitment and expertise in-house. Low cost (assuming personnel time is available) Disadvantages. May have biases that make it difficult to be objective. Experience limited to single organisation. Not always expert in WP market place and systems analysis and design. Comments. If you set up an in-house study team, make sure all users are represented: management, personnel and data processing staffs; authors and secretaries. Designate a lead, but keep everyone involved.

CONTINUED ...

FOOTER: MODERNISE OR NOT TODAY!

---

6. Alignment of Text

By default, text is displayed as **left-aligned** as it is typed, but alignment can also be centred, right-aligned or have alignment known as **Full Justification**. WP software provides features for left, right, centred and justified alignment.

(i) Left-aligned Text
This text is **left-aligned**:

Outdoor living in the countryside

(ii) Centred Text
Text that is centred is positioned an equal distance from the left and right margin. This text is **centred**:

McDonnell Enterprises

(iii) Right-aligned Text
When the right-aligned feature is turned on, the cursor is positioned at the right margin and the text aligns with the right margin as it is typed.
This text is **right-aligned**:

The sunshine breakfast

(iv) Justified Text
Justification means the insertion of extra space between words in lines of type, so that the left and right margins are even and smooth. When this feature is turned on, the text position on the line is adjusted as it is typed, so that the end result has the effect of the text evenly spaced across the line.
This text is **justified**:

A keen collector of quilts, chintz china and old fabrics, Nicola has used them throughout to give her home a wonderfully traditional look. 'I'm a collector of a lot of

(v) To Re-align Text (Unjustify)
To change the alignment from one type to another, e.g. from justified to centred. Select text, select Centred Alignment feature — text is re-aligned.

(vi) Ragged Margin
The opposite to the justified effect is Ragged Margin — a new line is started after the last word that fits in before the right margin — it gives an uneven line-ending effect to the margin as a whole.
This text has a **ragged-right margin**:

His home kitchen looks just as professional as a working one. To create an efficient workspace, Stewart has gone for a selection of smart, low-level stainless steel units a huge cooker and granite work surfaces.

TASK 18E

- Key in the following text; use an indented style with paragraph numbering and headers and footers.
- Save as 'Workload'.
- Print one copy on A4 portrait paper.

DEFINING YOUR WORKLOAD II

Most organisations which are considering WP equipment do some kinds of analysis or study. The reason for doing a WP study is simple: to identify the kind and amount of WP typing that needs to be done. The study process itself can range from the simple to the complex, depending largely on the complexity of the organisation. Not surprisingly, a two-person law office is easier to survey than as 135-member engineering firm.

As a general rule, the more rigorous the study, the more precise the final systems design will be. In a large organisation some kind of quantitative analysis is essential. In a small business, you can be somewhat more subjective.

GETTING STARTED

Whatever your approach to analysing your needs, there are some important first steps. In a large organisation, they are essential. A small business will also benefit from their discipline. The purpose is to reduce the office's natural resistance to change by removing as much mystery from WP as early as possible.

When you change the way an office does its work, you need to make sure the office will follow your lead. It is not enough to have a clear picture of the workload and to know that WP will solve your problems. You also need to have the full support of both management and staff.

(1½ line spacing)

CONTINUED ...

Footer: MODERNISE OR NOT TODAY!

(Change page numbering to: Page 11, 12 & 13)

---

7. Bold

The Bold command enables you to darken text.
Usually, you can use this command either by:
Using the **EMBOLDENING** command to turn on the feature, typing the text and using the **EMBOLDENING** command again to turn the feature off, or selecting (or highlighting the text) and using the **EMBOLDENING** command once.
Note: The word **emboldening** is in bold print.

8. Italics

The Italics command applies a *slanting* effect.
Usually, you can use this command either by:
Using the *ITALICS* command to turn on the feature, typing the text and using the *ITALICS* command again to turn the feature off, or selecting (or highlighting the text) and using the *ITALICS* command once.
Note: The word *ITALICS* is in italics.

9. Underlining (also referred to as 'Underscoring')

The Underlining command enables you to place a line underneath text.
Usually, you can use this command either by:
Using the Underlining command to turn on the feature, typing the text and using the Underlining command again to turn the feature off, or selecting the text and using the Underlining command once.
Note: The word Underlining is underlined.

10. Search and Replace

This feature allows the user to find data and replace it with other data by:
Keying in the text being sought and then — keying in the replacement text.
The user can then find the text, and replace one or all occurrences of the text.

TASK 18D

- Key in the following text; use bullets and hanging paragraphs.

- Set up a two-column format and create a header and footer for this page only.

- Save as 'WP 80s'.

- Print one copy on A4 portrait paper.

WORD PROCESSING IN THE '80'S

Word processors have revolutionised office life in the 1980's. They save time, increase efficiency and remove much drudgery from routine business communications. Everyone involved in office life - including secretaries, managers, lawyers, owners of businesses - needs to understand how word processors operate and what they can do.

This handbook takes readers step-by-step through word processing techniques and terminology. The text, accompanied by numerous illustrations, answers the key questions for non-experts:

What problems can word processing solve?
What are the pitfalls to avoid when buying a word processor?
How is the right machine selected?
How exactly does a word processor save time and money?
What is the best way to introduce word processing to a previously unautomated office?
What kind of staff training is required?

There are separate explanatory sections on related branches of office technology - data processing, electronic mail, typesetting. An extensive glossary of key word processing terms is always included in any word processing manual.

Times New Roman (14)

Revolutionary Office Technology

TASK 5A

- Open the file from Unit 4 — Task 4B — named 'Rustic Furniture MW'.

- Underline the phrase 'decorating rut'.

- Italicise all occurrences of both 'colour schemes' and 'soft furnishings'.

- Embolden each occurrence of the word 'room'.

- Insert two lines at the start of the document i.e. hit the Return key twice.

- On the first line type and centre the heading 'Revamp with Colour'.

- Use the Search and Replace command to make the following changes:

    Replace 'colour' with 'paint' also change 'coloured' to 'painted'.
    Replace 'changed regularly' with 'updated constantly'.
    Replace 'Louise' with 'Linda'.
    Replace 'contemporary' with 'fashionable'.
    Replace 'A career in fashion' with 'Enjoying a modern lifestyle'.
    Replace 'more than four times in' with 'each year for'.

- Fully justify the body of the document, i.e. excluding the heading.

- Create a page break; copy the document and paste it onto a new page — change the line spacing to double-line spacing for the copy.

- Move the cursor to the end of the document; hit the Return key twice — on the second line, type and right-align the phrase 'Branching out' in Times New Roman font and size 14.

- Save as 'Restoration' and close the file.

- Exit from both the WP software and the system before turning off the computer.

TASK 18C

- Key in the following text; use the bulleting facility of your WP software as indicated.
- Set up in a three-column format and put a line between the columns.
- Save as 'Computer Accessories'.
- Print one copy on A4 portrait paper.

COMPUTER ACCESSORIES — *to xxxx NT (24)*

VERBATIM
General Surface Cleaner

- 4 Bottles Cleaner
- 60 Lint Free Cloths
- Order 6 £5.95 ea

KODAK DISKS
- 5.25", DSDD
- Boxed in 10's
- Order 20   £4 per box
-

MANHATTAN
Mouse Pad
- Boxed
- Order 20   £1.75 ea

BULK DISKS
- 3.5", HD
- Order 500   42p ea

VERSACOMP
- Disk File Box
- 200 Capacity
- Lockable
- Stackable
- Order 5   £9.95 ea.

ZENIX
- Serial Mice
- Order 20   £8.95 ea.

BAFO
- 4:1 Auto Switch Box
- Parallel 4 in 1 out
- Order 5   £40 ea

BOSTON
- Optical Glass
- Filter 14"
- Anti-Static
- Anti-Glare
- UV Rays Reduced
- Order 5   £20 ea

SONY RE-WRITABLE OPTICAL DISKS
- Proven archival life of over 30 years
- Data integrity maintained even after 10 million erase/read/write cycles
- Resistant to adverse environmental conditions
- Packed in singles

FELLOWES HIGH CAPACITY DISKETTE TRAYS
- Lockable, hold 90 3 1/2" or 100 5 1/4" diskettes
- Dove grey and clear lid
- Rubber feet protect working surfaces
- Supplied with dividers and labels

ABA BOX FOR 3 1/2" DISKETTES
- Pivot lid and snap lock
- Single row complete with 4 dividers

REXEL DELUXE DISKETTE BOXES
- ABS anit-static plastic
- Lid can tilt or be removed to stack under base   *Times New Roman (14)*
- Includes five dividers with sliding tab indexes, plus
- A see-through identification label
- Smooth felt fabric feet
- Quality lock with two keys supplied

5 STAR EXPANDING FILE
- Quality laminated wipe-clean cover for extra durability
- Cloth reinforced gussets
- Strong plastic covered tabs for quick filing and identification 16 pockets indexed
- Size: Foolscap

VERSAPAK INTERNAL DISTRIBUTION WALLETS
- Durable PVC coated nylon pouch.
- Re-sealable velcro flay and address window Gussetted Wallet

---

VERSACOMP (IRL) LTD 141 Hawthorn Road Dublin 16   *brush script NT (24)*
Telephone: 01 876578   Fax: 01 873232 Mobile: 0871 54321

TASK 5B

- Open the file from Unit 4 — Task 4F — named 'Restaurant MW'.

- Insert two lines at the start of the document.

- On the first line type and centre in Arial font, size 16 the heading 'Cooking in the Kitchen'.

- Change the font of the paragraphs in the body of the document to Arial Narrow, size 12.

- Embolden each occurrence of the word 'cooking'.

- Italicise all occurrences of 'kitchen'.

- Underline the phrase 'East London flat'.

- Use the Search and Replace command to make the following changes:

  Replace 'chefs' with 'cooks'.
  Replace 'be commuting between the two' with 'relocate to Leeds'.
  Replace 'restaurant' with 'diner'.
  Replace 'a second' with 'another'.
  Replace 'Stewart' with 'Stuart'.
  Replace 'rushed off their feet' with 'burning the candle at both ends'.

- Fully justify the body of the document, i.e. excluding the heading.

- Cut the second paragraph and paste it below the third.

- Change the line spacing in the first paragraph to 1.5 spacing.

- Move the cursor to the end of the document; hit the Return key twice — on the second line, type and right-align the phrase 'Branching out'.

- Save the file using the existing filename and close it.

- Exit from both the WP software and the system before turning off the computer.

TASK 18B

- Key in the following text; use the paragraph numbering facility of your WP software to number main headings.
- Save as 'Ballyhoura'.
- Print one copy on A4 portrait paper.

Ballyhoura _ bold

Ballyhoura Country lies in Mid-Munster in Irelands' southern province, straddling Counties Cork, Limerick and Tipperary. The rugged beauty of the Ballyhoura hills and the Galtee mountains range to the south contrast with the lush rolling pastureland of one of Europe's richest dairyland areas, the Golden Vale, to the north.

Dbl Sp.

Places of Interest

i.   Ballyhoura Mountain Park

A natural park of woodland, rugged mountain and peat bog which is rich in wild plants and animal life. It offers marked walks, orienteering, and a fitness trail.

ii. Golf

The area has four uncrowded parklands courses - Mitchelstown and Charleville courses are 18 hole while Doneraile and Tipperary Golf Courses are 9 hole.

iii. Ryan's Honey Farm *(both)*

Fascinating honey farm and bee garden which is family run. It is located off the Palace Green to Emly road.

iv. Mitchelstown Caves:

4 Km off the Mitchelstown-Caher road, these caves, are among the finest limestones caves in Europe. Guided tours and coach parties welcome.

The Golden Vale: Europe's richest dairyland farms

Arial (16)

TASK 5C

- Open the file from Unit 3 — Task 3F — named 'Floral Blinds MW'.

- Embolden and underline both the phrases: 'wooden panelling' and 'pretty blue colour scheme'.

- Insert the text 'The expertise of House Beautiful specialists' on the first line — ensure there is a clear line between this heading and the body of the document.

- Embolden any occurrence of the phrase 'humble radiator' — use the Search and Replace command to speed up the location of the phrase.

- Italicise the phrase 'fond childhood memories'.

- Underline the phrase 'grandparent's farmhouse'.

- Use the Search and Replace command to make the following changes:

   Replace 'radiator' with 'rad'.
   Replace 'only five years old' with 'installed only a few years ago'.
   Replace 'bathroom's' with 'rest-room'.
   Replace 'suggested simply' with 'insisted on'.
   Replace 'Sue' with 'Susan'.
   Replace 'red-and-white gingham fabric' with 'more muted material'.

- Create a page break at the end of the document.

- Make a second copy of the document on the new page

- Change the line spacing within the document as follows:

   First paragraph: 1.5 spacing.
   Second paragraph: double-line spacing.

- Make a new paragraph at the point 'As the existing rest-room suite'.

- Move cursor to end of document; hit the Return key twice — on the second line, type and right-align the phrase 'Relax with a country-style look' — embolden, italicise and underline this phrase.

- Delete the last two sentences of the first paragraph.

- Print (if facilities permit) one copy of the first page and two of the second.

- Save as 'Gingham fabric' and close the file.

- Exit from both the WP software and the system before turning off the computer.

TASK 18A

- Key in the following document using the paragraph numbering facility of your WP software to number main headings.

- Save as 'West Cork'.

- Print one copy on A4 portrait paper.

West Cork — Script (36)

West Cork's scenery is among the most outstanding in the world, ranging from wooded valleys to desolate, rock strewn landscape, and a coastline dotted with islands. This is Ireland's most southerly area and its temperate climate encourages an abundance of flora and fauna from the rugged Beara Peninsula in the North, to Mizen Head, Ireland's most southerly point; there is plenty here for everybody. West Cork is rich in history and archaeology, and it has some of Europe's best fishing waters, and swimming facilities. enthusiasts of walking, golfing, sailing and fishing will find many activity, tuition and recreation centres here.

THINGS TO DO — Helv (14)

1. Walking

The wooded grounds of Castle Freke some 10 km south west of Clonakilty are well worth exploring. Its trees are broadleafed and coniferous. the name Castle Freke comes from the Freke family who acquired the area in the 17th century. It contains walks, car parks and scenic views.

2. Cycling

This is yet another way to enjoy West Cork's scenery to the full. Explore the hills and valleys in a leisurely fashion and imbibe all the countryside has to offer, including magnificent fuchsia and honeysuckle in the summer.

3. Horse Riding

Ireland has a reputation for its fine horses and in West Cork there are many horse riding facilities. Excellent riding centres have mounts to suit everyone from the beginner to the most experienced

4. Golfing

This area is a golfer's paradise. fine 9 and 18 hole golf courses are located amid some of the best scenery in Ireland.

uc

Remember in LARGE Roman Numerals

The craft centre in Skibbereen is not to be missed!

Arial (16)

TASK 5D

- Display the menu below on A5 paper.
- Centre and italicise the name of the restaurant 'Le Torc Restaurant', followed by the centred heading 'Special Dinner Menu: £19.99'.
- Centre each line of the menu as shown below, and italicise the names of the accompanying sauces.
- Save as 'Le Torc' and print one copy.

Steamed Fresh Mussels *in a White Wine Sauce*
Melon and Orange Cocktail *with Peppermint*
Smoked Mackerel *with Cream Cheese Pâté*
Golden Cheese & Leek Potato Cakes *with a Cream Sauce*
Dingle Bay Seafood Chowder
Cream of Vegetable Soup

Steamed Fillet of Salmon *with a Champagne Sauce*
Baked Fresh Sole *with a Prawn Sauce*
Grilled Fillets of Cod *with Chive Cream Sauce*
Roast Breast of Chicken *with an Orange Sauce*
Pan Fried Pork Cutlets *with Sage and Apple Sauce*
Irish Sirloin Steak *with Garlic Butter or Red Wine Sauce*

All dishes served with Potatoes & an assortment of fresh vegetables

Apple and Blackberry Crumble
Profiteroles *with Hot Chocolate Sauce*
Fresh Fruit Pavlova
Rich Chocolate Mousse
Bread and Butter Pudding

Tea or Coffee

Guidelines

1. Bullets/Numbering

Bullet points are used to emphasise a point and can be used instead of numbers to list items. A bullet point is a full stop which appears at the left of the typing line. A variety of different styles of bullet points can be used with WP software.

TASK 5E

- Display the menu below, as suggested.

- Use the font type Algerian for the title 'Menu', size 18.

- Save as 'Wild Mushroom Menu MW' and print one copy on A5 paper.

Menu

**Trio of Seasonal Melon with Midori
& Creme Fraiche**

* * *

or

* * *

**Savoury Pancake filled with Mussels,
Prawns & Salmon with a Dill,
Prawn & Cognac Cream**

* * *

Wild Mushroom Consomme Cheese Straw

* * *

or

* * *

Cream of Chicken & Sweetcorn Soup

* * *

Roast Leg of Lamb with Mint Sauce

* * *

**Dauphinoise Potatoes
Roast Potatoes
Selection of Five Green Vegetables**

* * *

**Baileys Cream Profiteroles & Warm
Chocolate Sauce**

* * *

Tea / Coffee & Mint Chocolates

Unit 18

Bullets

Paragraph Numbering

TASK 5F

- Key in the text below — use a left-aligned tab to indent each paragraph by five spaces for the indented effect.

- Make the suggested changes.

- Save as 'Hardware Store' and print one copy on A4 paper.

---

12 March 1994

Mr Robert Young
Managing Director
Hickey's Hardware Store
Kenilworth
Warwickshire

Dear Sir

Ref. 89/765/BG3F

I hv today received another letter from yr local branch manager, Mr. D Smith, who again has failed to mt my request for my microwave to be satisfactorily repaired or replaced. Technically, I appreciate that it was one week out of its guarantee when this particular fault developed. In view of the fact that I endured so many difficulties w this cooker during the first twelve months & that as I am such a loyal client the least I wd have expected was this guarantee to be extended to include this recent fault.

NP

I wd appreciate an early reply.

Yours faithfully

Dolly Walsh

Change to: Indented style

Change to Arial (10) font

SEARCH & REPLACE

Find	Replace with
hv	have
another letter	a note,
yr	your
Smith	Walsh
mt	meet
w	with
&	and
wd	would
first twelve months	last year
endured so many difficulties	experienced so many problems
loyal client	good customer

* Create a Page break here. Make a copy of revised document on second page. Change font to Times New Roman (12). Re-address letter to: Mr Simon Frost, O'Donovan's Crescent, Donnybrook, Dublin 4.

TASK 17D

- Create the following document.
- Proofread and save as 'DSP009'.
- Print four copies.

Gill & Macmillan Publishers Goldenbridge Inchicore Dublin 8 — Arial (16) — **Script (28)**

Tel 01 531005   Fax 01 541688

NEW BOOKS AUTUMN 1995 — *algeria (28)*

Please pick from the list below current titles that may be requested for inspection

ORDER FORM — *Ms Dialog (12)*

— *algeria (12)*

INSPECTION COPIES

Book Antique (12)

Germany from Napoleon to Bismarck 1800-1866 Thomas Nipperdey — *Helv (12)*	The Darling of My Heart 2,000 Years of Irish Love Writing Laurence Flanagan
On the Move Coras Iompair Eireann 1945-1995 Micheal O Riain	Favourite Irish Name for Children The Top 200 Laurence Flanagan
The Tipp Revival The Keating Years Seamus Leahy	Return of the Great Goddess Burleigh Muten, ed
Thou Shalt Not Kill Edited by Kevin O'Connor	New Way of Life A Practical Guide to Managing Arthritis and Chronic Pain Loraine Condon
Small Differences Irish Catholics and Irish Protestants 1815-1922 Donald Harman Akenson	On Becoming a Counsellor Second Edition A basic Guide for Non-Professional Counsellors Eugene Kennedy

---

Please send me an inspection copy of the Titles that I have ticked. I understand that Books on approval have to be returned within 3 days of delivery, otherwise I pay for in full immediately.

Monotype Corsiva (16)

Signed:_____   Position:_____   Date:_____

School/College:_____   Address:_____

_____

SECTION TWO

Additional Word Processing Techniques

TASK 17C

- Create the following document, as designed below.

- Proofread and save as 'MM001'.

M E M O R A N D U M

Date: 17/07/95

To: Each Staff Member

From: Mr John Roche, General
              Manager.

Subject: Election of Union
              Official

All Staff Members are now being circularised regarding the appointment of the Shop Steward for the coming year. Please tick in order of preference your choice of candidate.

Mr John Welch Accounts Clerk	☐	Mr Tim Rice Assistant Manager	☐
Ms Janice Cooke Secretary	☐	Ms Judy Hoare Secretary	☐
Mr Roger Lynch Cashier	☐	Mr Ray Doyle Accountant	☐
Mr Jim Kerins Clerk	☐	Mr Jim Cooney Cashier	☐

Please complete and return to me not later than July 22, 1995.

NAME: _____   **RSI No.** ☐☐☐☐☐☐☐☐

Dept: _____   **Date:** _____

17/07/95   *Confidential*

UNIT 6

Indented Text

Tabs

Clip Art

Memorandums

TASK 17B

- Create the following display.
- This is an ad which is to be placed in the local newspaper and includes a space for a photograph.
- Proofread, save appropriately and print one copy.

GRADE A — *algerian (18)*

THE BERKLEY COURT HOTEL
Rochestown Road Cork

Tel. No. 021 5443243
Telex No. 4323212

Helv (14) Italic

Faces South - Adjoining New Link Road

Ballroom	*Dancing Every Night*
Crazy Golf	*TV & Video All Rooms*
Pool Tables	*Telephone*
Heated Swimming Pool	*Residents' Bar*

24 Hour Service

Choose from:
Full Board
B&B only
B&B & Evening Meal
Chef with European Awards
Off Season: £89 per Day (Full Board)
£35 B&B
£50 other

2"

5"

P H O T O
of
Hotel

Group Discount

Special Golden Age Rates

Footlight MT (14)

Berkley Court Hotel now included in: AA Failte Guide

Arial (18) Bold

<u>General Manager: Mr Liam Rice</u>

Guidelines

1. Indented Text

An **indented block** of text is typed with the left and right margins much wider than the rest of the document. (Indented Paragraph is described in Unit 5.)
Hanging paragraphs are typed with the first line starting at a pre-set point nearer to the left margin than the rest of the paragraph.

2. Tabs

Tab Stop: A position you set for placing and aligning text on a page.
Four tab types are: **Left, Centered, Decimal** and **Right**.
Left: Text is aligned on the left as in the example below:

Jack	Jim	Joe
Rita	May	Alice

Note: Centered, right and decimal tabs are studied in a later Unit as are Leader dots.

3. Clip Art

Word processing Windows software includes a wide variety of pictures, photographs, sounds, and video clips that can be inserted into your documents. Within Word for Windows, for example, the Insert Picture Clip Art option is used. Clip Art when selected, can be moved around the screen so that it isn't placed on text.

4. Memorandums

Some companies may design their own personal house style, but generally, a typical layout for a memo would be as follows:

- The heading 'MEMORANDUM' is centred and typed in bold capitals.
- **'To'** is typed three lines below the heading.
- The **addressees'** names and job titles should be keyed in as indicated in the memo example on page 45.
- The **date** is typed on the same line as the 'To' using a left-aligned tab at least three inches from the right margin.
- Allow one clear line after the addressees and enter **'Copies'**; align the addresses with the earlier addressees.
- The **'From'** line should be typed one line space below the last recipient of copies.
- The **reference** number is entered on the same line aligned with the date above.
- Allow three clear lines after the **'Ref'** line before keying in the centred emboldened **heading**.
- Paragraphs are blocked with one clear line between paragraphs.
- Any enclosure is indicated by the word **'Enc'** (followed by the relevant number if there is more than one enclosure) — this is typed below the last line of the memo.

FORM 1

Ms Shirley Fawcett of Beverley Downs, Wilton, Cork rang Malahide Yacht Club and requested that a Cadet application form be filled in on her behalf. She was born on the 22 February 1954. Her home tel. no. is 021 34765. She is a nurse at the Regional Hospital, Cork, and her work number is 021 37653. She wants Cadet class. To date she has not been a crew member with anybody. Committee Members: John Collins and Kieran Fitzgerald both know her. She is a member of Bishopstown Tennis Club.

FORM 2

Doctor Jim Long of Model Farm Road, Cork, wants to become a Cadet. His surgery is at his home. He has crewed for O'Donoghue's boat and wants now to be registered under Dinghy Class. Jim Burton and Tim O'Leary, who are Committee Members, have known him for many years. He was born on 23 February 1948 and his telephone numbers are: home: 02147643 and work: 021 54443. He is currently a member of Cork Golf Club.

FORM 3

Mr Con Mullane of O'Downey Crescent, Glenbrook, Co Cork, (tel. no. 021 43232) was born 12 May, 1956. He works as an accountant at Sheehan & Co, Patrick's Hill, Cork: tel. no. 021 87443. He crewed last summer with Noel Rice & Co. He wants to be registered under Cadet Class. He knows Jim Burton. He is a keen member of Dolphin Rugby Club.

FORM 4

Mr Dick Rice (born 2-3-1932) is a Tax Inspector with the Tax Office, Sullivan's Quay, Cork: tel. no. 021 74344. He resides at Diamond Hill, Monkstown, Cork: tel. no. 021 34324. He is already a member of Sunday's Well Lawn & Tennis Club. He wants to be included in Cadet Class as he is an occasional crew member with John Foley. He doesn't know anybody on the Committee.

Example of a Memo

MEMORANDUM

To: John Welch, Stores Manager   1 April 2000
            Tricia Long, Supervisor
            Ria Leech

Copies: Lena Cotter, Accountant

From: Kate Mulhaire, General Manager   **Ref:** STD/JK

Grattan Street Carnival

The 4th Annual Grattan Street Carnival will be held this year from Friday, 7 June to Sunday, 9 June. Many new interesting items are included. See the attached brochure for details.

Enc

TASK 17A

- Design the following form; use the Lines and Box facilities of your word processing program.

- Flag input points appropriately and save as 'FM890'.

- This skeleton form can be retained for future use.

- Turn overleaf. Use the Form Filling facility of your word processing software to fill in copies of this form from the information given.

M A L A H I D E   Y A C H T   C L U B

No:

Date:

MEMBERSHIP NOMINATION FORM

CATEGORY

STUDENT

NAME

CADET

DATE OF BIRTH

HOME

ADDRESS

Telephone

BUSINESS

ADDRESS

Telephone

Notes

The Proposer's attention is drawn to the follwoing rule:

Rule 2A:- The Proposer of anynew member shallb e liable for his/her entry fee, and first year's subscription.

Age reckkoning as on January 1st

Occupation _____

Clubs (if any) _____

Cadet/Dinghy Class _____

Crew Member with _____

Members of Committe to whom candidate is known:

_____

Candidate's Signature:_____

We believe that the abovae Candidate is a fit and proper person to be admitted to the Club and would be welcomed by exdsitng members.

TASK 6A

- Create the following blocked-style Memorandum — display as suggested. **MEMORANDUM, From, To, Date** and **All Staff** are in bold.

- A left-aligned tab will be required.

- **MW** represents the initials of the person who dictated the document, while **JH** are the initials of the typist in the line 'MW/JH'.

- **Enc** means one item is enclosed; two enclosures would read 'Enc 2'.

MEMORANDUM

From   John Rice, Personnel Department

To   **All Staff**

Date   1 May 2002

LANGUAGE FLUENCY

Please note that as from week beginning, Monday, 25 June, the Language Course in German will resume. It is expected that everybody will make the effort to be there for 6 consecutive weeks at 7.30 pm. The venue as usual will be Annex 7. I enclose Content Sheet.

MW/JH

Enc

Guidelines

1. Forms

A standard document can be designed to create a form. Entry points for the inputting of varying data can be marked with a relevant code or symbol.

Use the appropriate command from the word processing programs to find these pre-set codes/symbols and replace them with data.

TASK 6B

- Using the same memo style as before, create the memorandum below sent by Gerry Thornley, the Irish Times Sports Commentator to all Irish Times readers on Saturday, 27 May, 2000.

Munster haven't had a bad one yet this season and they're unlikely to start now. A slight problem is that Northampton might well produce a big 80 minute performance as well, which would possibly be the first Munster will will have run into. As Pat Lam, their fulminating Samoan number eight pointed out yesterday, the two finalists probably have the best team spirit of any two sides in the competition.

Unit 17

Forms

Creation of Lines

TASK 6C

• Key in the following memo; use the earlier examples as a guide.

Memo from John Barton, Arklow, Co Wicklow to Kaye O'Regan, Facilitator, Film Review.

Date is 23 July 2000.

Ref **JB/KL/BHT/4**

Heading to be used is: Edward Norton the hip new director of *Keeping the Faith*

Some facts on the above, which you might find interesting.

Edward Norton has average height, average build, average, slightly pale looks and has a dry, self-deprecating style of speaking.

In the four years since making his movie debut, Norton has been in six films, received two Oscar nominations, and been hailed as the great white hope of his acting generation. Some of those movies have been better than others, all have been interesting at least. Anyway, the 30-year-old actor has emerged from each one with his reputation enhanced.

TASK 16B

- Create the following document in columns.

- Use the Thesaurus facility to replace the words combination 'simultaneously and resist'.

- Use the Protected Spaces facility of your word processor to protect 'Windows 95'.

- Set up the Widow/Orphan facility.

- Create footnotes and endnotes.

- Proofread and save as 'Micro95'.

MICROSOFT OFFICE 95

Italics

Our look at a beta version of Microsoft's new Win95 - ready software suite reveals much to make the competition nervous

The gloves are coming off. not content to throw the single punch of Windows Office 95 - expected to ship in Ireland in September after so many months - Microsoft is winding up to deliver a roundhouse in the form of Office for Windows Office 95.

The combination of a new version of Windows shipping almost simultaneously with a new Windows Office 95 - optimised version of what is already the best - selling office suite is going to be temptation many Windows users won't be able to resist.

STRONGER APPLICATIONS — (Italics)

~~At first glance,~~ the new features in Windows' Office 95 applications may seem disappointing, because you won't find long lists of new power features such as when pivot features such as when pivot tables were added to Excel or tables were added to Word. the improvements in this version are a bit more subtle.

For starters, all applications are now 32-bit instead of 16-bit. That won't make you type faster, but it will mean faster opening, paging and saving of files and Excel recalculation speeds that will be about 50 per cent faster, according to Microsoft.

Second, the applications now support true multi-threading. Again, the benefits are limited but real. Specifically printing operations now run on their own thread, which means you can get back to work quicker, and queries in Access reportedly will also have their own thread.

Create: Footnotes: ① "bill Gates is founder of Microsoft"
② "see Windows 95 Launch - TBD .95".

Create End Note: "Microsoft office for Value"

TASK 6D

- Display effectively the following menu.
- Save as 'Erin Lodge MW'.

Erin Lodge Hotel
Lunch Menu
Soup of the Day
Salmon Mousse
Egg Mayonnaise

Roast Stuffed Spring Chicken
Steamed Whiting and Lemon Sauce | Bold
Indian Curry and Rice

Apple Tart and Cream
Fresh Fruit Salad

Coffee or Tea

London is stituated on the River ~~Barrow~~ *Thames,* [in what is called the London basin] (This "basin" is really more like a shallow saucer with a floor of clay resting upon chalk. ~~t~~he Thames, known to Londoners as "the river", winds its way through this saucer, dividing London into north and south. *uc* ~~Thames, known to Londoners as "the river", divides London into north and south.~~ *dd*

NP [The Romans probably built the first wall; then came, the Old London Bridge, ~~built in stone and begun in 11765, then came, the Old London Bridge,~~ built in stone and begun in 11765.[3]

The Centre of Government:

[on the north side of the Thames]

Today, Charing Cross is taken to be the centre of London. ~~A round it are the buildings which show that London is centre of London.~~ around it are the buildings *uc* which show that London is the centre of Britain's government. [The Queen lives in *UP* Buckingham Palace for much of the year, but there are other royal palaces in London *#* as well. ~~St for much of he year, but there are other royal palaces in London as well.~~ St. James's Palace, Kensington Place, the Tower, Clarence House, all belong to the *NP* sovereign. [If you stand beside the Houses of Parliament, you can look down the street called Whitehall flanked by the main government offices, Off Whitehall is a narrow, rather dull-looking street called Downing Street. [⊕]

[including the Home Office]

The West End

west

[Ω] West of Charing Cross is the ~~East~~ End. In this area are to be found stores and shops in streets such as Oxford Street and Bond Street. This part of London also contains many hotels and above all theatres. No city in the world has more to offer people who love the theatre than has London. ~~No city in the world has more to offer people who love the theatre than has London.~~ [North of Oxford Street is London's *NP* smallest building, the 620-foot Post Office Tower, which is a centre for radio and *UP* telephone communications. [Trafalgar Square [Regent Street]

Trafalgar Square, known for its fountains, pigeons and the towering Nelson's column, is close to Charing Cross. It is overlooked by the National Gallery.

The Growth of London

hills

London was first built on two low, gravel-topped ~~mountains~~ on the north bank of the Thames. ~~Also, although~~ the river was just shallow enough to ford (to cross on foot), *uc* its south side was marshy and enemies found it difficult to launch a surprise attack. So a settlement grew up on these two hills, and this became the town which the Romans called Londinium. *On one of these hills St Paul's Cathedral now stands and on the other, the bank of England.*

---

[3] Removed in 1832 and replaced by another about 30 metres up stream built by John Rennie.
[⊕] See Encyclopaedia Britannica
[Ω] See London A-Z } *End Notes*

Footnote ↑

TASK 6E

- Create the following document.
- Centre and embolden the main heading.
- Use the left-aligned tab to calculate the position of the text.
- Save as 'Websites MW'.

WEBSITES RUN BY SPORTS INTERNET

Aston Villa	Sheffield Wednesday	Coventry City
Southampton	Everton	Sunderland
Leeds United	West Ham United	Leicester City
Wimbledon	Middlesbrough	Manchester City
Newcastle United	Chelsea	Manchester United

TASK 16A

- Key in the document below; proofread, correct where necessary and make the changes as indicated.

- Please use 1" (2.5 cm) for left and right margins.

- Use ragged margins.

- Insert text under 'Trafalgar Square' and indent 2" from the margin in order to leave space for the photograph to be attached at a later time.

- Set up specified footnotes and endnotes.

- Use the Widow/Orphan facility.

- Centre numbering in the footer.

- Use the Thesaurus facility to replace stone, streets and enemies.

- Save as 'London01', and print once on A4 paper.

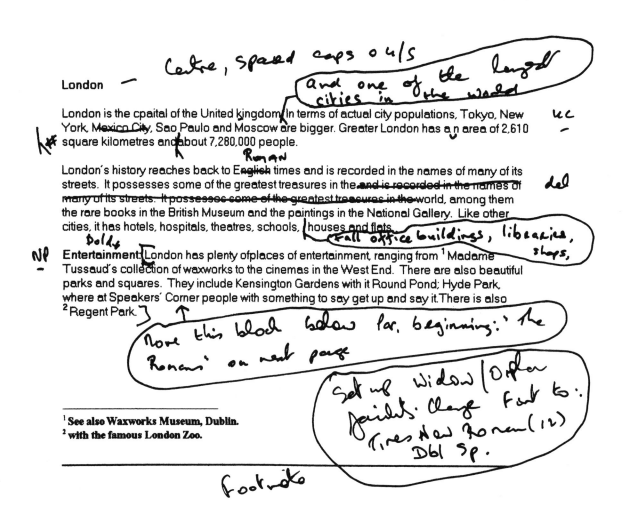

London — *Centre, spaced caps o u/s*

and one of the largest cities in the world

London is the cpaital of the United kingdom. In terms of actual city populations, Tokyo, New York, Mexico City, Sao Paulo and Moscow are bigger. Greater London has a n area of 2,610 square kilometres and about 7,280,000 people. *uc*

Roman

London's history reaches back to English times and is recorded in the names of many of its streets. It possesses some of the greatest treasures in the. and is recorded in the names of many of its streets. It possesses some of the greatest treasures in the world, among them the rare books in the British Museum and the paintings in the National Gallery. Like other cities, it has hotels, hospitals, theatres, schools, houses and flats. *del*

Tall office buildings, libraries, shops,

Dolly

NP Entertainment: London has plenty of places of entertainment, ranging from [1] Madame Tussaud's collection of waxworks to the cinemas in the West End. There are also beautiful parks and squares. They include Kensington Gardens with it Round Pond; Hyde Park, where at Speakers' Corner people with something to say get up and say it. There is also [2] Regent Park.

Move this block below par. beginning: ' The Romans' on next page

Set up Widow/Orphan points. Change font to: Times New Roman (12) Dbl sp.

[1] See also Waxworks Museum, Dublin.
[2] with the famous London Zoo.

footnote

TASK 6F

- Create the following document.
- Centre and italicise the main heading.
- Use the left-aligned tab to calculate the position of the text.
- Save as 'Stars MW'.

HEAVENLY HOMES

Cancer	Leo	Virgo
Libra	Scorpio	Sagittarius
Capricorn	Aquarius	Gemini
Aries	Taurus	Pisces

Guidelines

1. Footnotes/Endnotes

Footnotes and endnotes explain, comment on, or provide references for the text in a document. You can include both footnotes and endnotes in the same document, for example, use footnotes for detailed comments and endnotes for a list of sources.

Place the cursor at the point in the document where the footnote/endnote is to be inserted and use the appropriate command. A symbol is inserted at this point and usually a pane opens and you are allowed to key in the required text.

2. Protected Spaces

If you wish to ensure that a group of words, or characters, are not separated or divided at the end of a line when the system wraps words on to the next line, you may use a facility known as 'Protected Space'. Most word processing programs provide a command for this purpose.

3. Widow/Orphan Lines

A **widow** line is the first line of a paragraph of text that is separated from the rest of the paragraph. A widow line appears at the bottom of the page, whereas the rest of the paragraph appears at the top of the next page.

An **orpha**n line is the last line of a paragraph of text that is separated from the rest of the paragraph. An orphan line appears at the top of the page, whereas the rest of the paragraph appears at the bottom of the previous page.

4. Thesaurus

This is a collection of words with the same meaning. Most word processing programs provide a command to find synonyms to match existing words.

TASK 6G

- Create the following document.
- Centre and italicise the main heading.
- Use the left-aligned tab to calculate the position of the text.
- Save as 'TV Addicts MW'.

LISTINGS FOR TV ADDICTS

Jenny Jones	Pokemon	Mega Babies
Stargate	Veronica's Closet	Friends
The Simpsons	Coppers	South park
New York Undercover	Long Play	Antiques Watch
Emmerdale	You TV	Home and Away
Renegade	Spotlight	Fish

Unit 16

Footnotes/Endnotes

Protected Spaces

Widow/Orphan Lines

Thesaurus

TASK 6H

- Create the following document.
- Display the main heading, as suggested.
- Use the left-aligned tab to calculate the position of the text.
- Save as 'Anniversaries MW'

Anniversaries - SPACED CAPS + BOLD

First	Cotton	Fifteenth	Crystal
Second	Paper	Twentieth	China
Third	Leather	Twenty-fifth	Pearl
Fifth	Wooden	Thirtieth	Silver
Seventh	Tin	Fortieth	Ruby
Tenth	Woollen	Fiftieth	Golden
Twelfth	Silk	Sixtieth	Diamond

TASK 15D

Those who were not there to witness the event first hand might now have the wrong impression. They might have thought that the "stern warning" on Irish inflation delivered by Mr Wim Duisenberg at the Financial Services Industry Association annual dinner recently would have produced sharp intakes of breath, a frantic media scrum, consternation behind official closed doors, market traders screaming orders into mobile phones and other such clinched behavioural responses.

The curious thing is that the event passed almost unnoticed at the time, certainly judging by the diners, who didn't blink a poker eyelid at the disapproving mention of "pro-cyclical fiscal policy".

Many had heard it before from the European Central Bank, of course. It was sort of noticeable in a "no news" way that nothing happened to Irish stocks either. Not a tick, upwards or downwards, was ascribed to the remarks from the ECB president.

Writing afterwards in this newspaper, Dr Dan McLaughlin of ABN Amro stockbrokers asked how people would view the chairman of the Federal Reserve, Mr Alan Greenspan, giving out to Rhode Island about its "domestic" inflation rate, a matter of equally low significance for US inflation as the Irish rate is for the euro zone.　　**(25 wpm)**

Another stockbroker and I mused on a separate track. Imagine if the speaker at the Financial Services Industry Association dinner had been Mr Greenspan instead of Mr Duisenberg. Imagine he had delivered the exact same speech. The Irish equity market could, would, have been walloped. Maybe there's the solution to the troubles of Irish companies battling against a scepticism about the Irish economy: invite Mr Greenspan to the next association dinner.　　**(35 wpm)**

To be serious, there is a discernible element of Mr Duisenberg being scapegoated for the euro's woes. A heroes and villains analysis of central bankers is obviously superficial. The market moving weight Mr Greenspan enjoys arises not alone from his judgments and the Fed's longer track record, but from very different institutional and policy contexts in the US.

The message Mr Duisenberg delivered here was not remarkable, new, or directly prescriptive. There was a much wider issue in play to do with Ireland's standing in Europe and the political battle over the euro project.　　**(45 wpm)**

We have always told ourselves that we have been good Europeans cynically some say while we were looking for ever-greater support form the EU. Now, the tide is turning. We are set to become a net contributor to the EU budget.

Right now the inflation difference between Ireland and the rest of the EU is being seized upon as evidence of the failure of the euro project, particularly by British eurosceptics.　　**(50 wpm)**

TASK 6I

- Create the following document.
- Display the main heading, as suggested.
- Use the left-aligned tab to calculate the position of the text.
- Save as 'Furniture MW'.

Furniture — U/S

Bookcases	Typists' Desks	Upholstered Chairs	Static Pedestals	Storage Unit [CASE]
Typists' Desks	Oak Cabinet	Printer Table	Reception Table	Lamp Cabinet
Manager Chair	Stacking Chair	Pine Workstation	Split-Level Unit	Bookcase
Executive Chairs	Filing Cabinets	Telephone Tables	Telephone Table	Split-Level Unit
Workstation	Printer Cart BMY	Pedestal Unit	VDU Table	Hill Furniture
Mobile CPU Stand	Rose Bureau	Display Unit	Unit Triangle	Tall Storage Unit
Wardrobes	Cabinets	Filing Cabinet	Photocopier Table	Double Desk

TASK 15C

- Key in the passage below — figures in the right margin are not to be typed — these figures indicate the lines on which specified speeds are reached.

- Use double-line spacing and leave adequate margins.

- Type your name at the top of each sheet.

- Save as 'Accuracy3'.

An even more sober picture can be painted using the employment data from the Labour Force and Quarterly National Household Surveys based on International Labour Organisation labour force definitions. These sources reveal an even higher employment growth rate than is shown in the table and imply that the rate of growth of output per worker was only 2.4 per cent over the period 1990-99, falling to less than 1.5 per cent over the last three years.

Thus more than half of the growth of GNP in the 1990s has been due to the growth of employment, and in recent years this proportion has risen to over three-quarters. The conclusion seems inescapable. To the extent that there is a "Celtic Tiger" or an Irish economic "miracle", it has taken the form of an astonishing growth in the numbers at work rather than a surge in labour productivity.

These trends have far-reaching implications. In the first place, the continued growth of living standards depends on improvements in productivity rather than on rapid growth in the labour force. Living standards in Ireland enjoyed an extra boost during the 1990s due to the rising employment/population ratio but this is a once-off phenomenon reflecting rising labour force participation rates and the changing age structure of the population. The underlying trends imply that much more modest rates of improvement in living standards will be achieved in the long run. **(25 wpm)**

Secondly, the level of employment is most unlikely to continue to grow at the rates recorded in recent years. A rate of employment growth of about 1.5 per cent would seem the highest sustainable over the medium term. Combining this with the current rate of growth of labour productivity implies that the rate of growth of GNP will fall to the region of 4 per cent a year. **(35 wpm)**

The relatively unimpressive rate of growth of labour productivity revealed in the GNP data contrasts with the spectacular productivity gains being recorded in many industrial sectors. But it is easy to lose sight of the fact that these sectors account for a relatively small and declining proportion of the Irish labour force.

In the longer run, the rate of growth in living standards will increasingly depend on improvements in the efficiency of the rest of the economy, especially in the dominant service sectors. This challenge deserves to receive much more attention than it has to date. **(45 wpm)**

We have every reason to feel proud of the extraordinary rates of growth of output and employment that have been recorded during the 1990s. **(50 wpm)**

TASK 6J

- Create the following document.
- Display the main heading as suggested, and underline headings where indicated.
- Use the left-aligned tab to calculate the position of the text.
- Set the line spacing to double-line spacing.
- Save as 'Typewriters MW'.

<u>TYPEWRITERS</u> – TRAINING CENTRE – Section 8   ⟋ Centre

<u>Brand</u>	<u>Code</u>	<u>Type</u>
IBM Wheelwriter	JG 3458	Electronic
Olympia Electric	KL 897	Electric
Facit	OP 642	Manual
Adler	YT 9011	~~Manual~~ Electronic
Royal	YT 6542	Manual
IBM Selectric	BT 7985	Electric – Correcting Ribbon
~~IBM Selectric~~ Adler	TB 76421	Electric

(Rule)

TASK 15B

- Key in the passage below — figures in the right margin are not to be typed — these figures indicate the lines on which specified speeds are reached.
- Use double-line spacing and leave adequate margins.
- Type your name at the top of each sheet.
- Save as 'Accuracy2'.

The release of official national income estimates for 1999 affords an opportunity to assess the 1995 in perspective. In doing so, it is timely to draw attention to a feature of the boom that has received too little attention to date, namely the extraordinary growth of employment and the relatively modest rate of increase of output per worker.

Over the period 1990-99, real Gross National Product (GNP) increased at an annual average rate of 6.5 per cent. (GNP excludes the profits of multinational national companies remitted abroad and may understate the growth rate, but Gross Domestic Product [GDP] overstates it due to the effects of transfer pricing.) The growth rate climbed to over 8 per cent a year in the second half of the 1990s.

In 1999 the volume of national production was 70 per cent higher than it had been in 1990. This record has no parallel in other countries. In keeping with the tendency of Irish commentators to focus on the growth of total output, these figures are not adjusted for the increase in the number of people at work.

Between 1990 and 1999, the numbers at work grew at an annual average rate of 3.3 per cent and by more than 5 per cent since 1994. There were 34 per cent more people at work in 1999 than at the start of the decade.

These are truly amazing growth rates, more than twice those recorded in the US, which is often cited as an exemplary "jobs machine". Failure to take account of the growth in employment risks misunderstanding the essence of the current boom. From many perspectives, the growth of GNP per capita or per employed person is a more meaningful indicator than the growth of GNP. **(25 wpm)**

A simple measure of the rate of growth of labour productivity is obtained by adjusting the growth rate of output for the rate of employment growth. **(35 wpm)**

(A more refined measure would allow for changes in hours worked, but this is not a major consideration because the proportion of part-time jobs has not increased dramatically.)

When account is taken of the remarkable growth of employment, we see that the rate of growth of GNP per person employed averaged 2.7 per cent over the 1990s; by the end of the decade it had fallen to about half this.

Even if GDP is used to measure output, the annual average growth rate over the 1990s only rises to 3.3 per cent. These rates are respectable but not exceptional by international standards. They are higher than the rate of productivity growth achieved in the larger EU economies in recent years, but significantly below that currently reported in the US. **(50 wpm)**

TASK 6K

- Create the following document.
- Display the main heading, as suggested.
- Use the left-aligned tab to calculate the position of the text.
- Set the line spacing to double-line spacing.
- Save as 'CV MW'.

CURRICULUM VITAE ← (spaced caps + bold)

Name: Miss Marian Foster

Address: 2 Upper John Street
Rosslare
Co Wexford

Leave 1.5" Space for insertion of Photograph

Date of Birth: 1 June 1975

Examinations passed: Junior Certificate: 1991 – 9 Honours
Leaving Certificate: 1994 - 6 Honours

Schools Attended: Rosslare Community School: 1989-1994
St Joseph's Girls' National School: 1980-1988

Hobbies/Interests: Music, Reading, Tennis, Hockey, Sailing

Referees: Mr John Bilk, Principal, Rosslare Community School
Rev Fr John Dorgan, C.C., Rosslare

Work Experience: [Put the most recent first] Part-time Work in KC Chipper: 1991-1992
Saturday Work in Roches' Stores: 1993
Work Experience in Cohalan & Son Solicitors South Mall
Cork: 2 weeks in July 1995

Further Education: Secretarial Course: Karton Commercial College
Subjects: Typewriting Shorthand Commerce Audio-
Typing Commercial Arithmetic Computer Studies

Achievements: Student of the Year: 1990
Head Girl: 1993-1994

Signed: _____ Date: _____

TASK 15A

- Key in the passage below — figures in the right margin are not to be typed — these figures indicate the lines on which specified speeds are reached.

- Use double-line spacing and leave adequate margins.

- Type your name at the top of each sheet.

- Save as 'Accuracy1'.

Last week, while tennis balls were flying back and forth at the 2000 US Open, it was IBM that was keeping score. In its ninth year of partnership with the United States Tennis Association; IBM had an Internet group and a scoring room beneath the Arthur Ashe and Louis Armstrong stadiums in Flushing, New York.

It aimed to replicate the real-time scoring systems that it provided to local audiences at the Australian Open, French Open and Wimbledon by handling all the US Tennis Association's technical needs on-site but this time, it took the technology worldwide.

No doubt it was good preparation for IBM's role as worldwide information technology partner at the Olympic Games in Sydney. IBM has just received the patent on what it calls a Digital Video Wall and it will use this in Sydney to provide eight video windows of the sports action on a single Web page.

The US Open ran from August 26th to September 10th and, for its duration, IBM designed and implemented the United States Tennis Association's website, produced match-in-progress reports and provided statistical information, such as scores, to the media. **(25 wpm)**

About 10,000 people checked into the wireless site after the first week of the tournament, an IBM spokesman said.

Also this year, US Open Daily, a live program streamed exclusively on the website, captured the atmosphere of the event. The half-hour, magazine-style show originated from various locations around the grounds of the United States Tennis Association's National Tennis Center and gave website visitors a taste of what it was like to actually be there, with video features, interviews with players, and a behind-the-scenes look at the US Open. **(35 wpm)**

Fans had a chance to send e-mail to the show for questions and comments each day. They could also register on the site to receive a daily up-date via e-mail and, by controlling four robotic cameras from their PCs, they could pan, zoom and take a snapshot.

The chairman and chief executive officer of IBM, talked about using the Internet for business at Comdex in 1995, "it was a very lonely place back then", said Mr John Patrick, vice-president of Internet technology at IBM.

A lot has changed in just five years. Now, the idea of pervasive computing is one that IBM estimates will become a $230 billion market in the next few years and IBM hopes to capture one-third of it. **(45 wpm)**

Today about 95 per cent of Web pages are wired through a personal computer and browser. "That percentage will drop to between 45 per cent and 50 per cent in a couple of years," Mr Peter said, "not because PCs will decline but because other devices will grow". **(50 wpm)**

Unit 7

Tabs

Leader Characters

Unit 15

Word Processing — Speed and Accuracy Tests

Guidelines

1. Tabs

The other tab types are **Center**, **Right** and **Decimal**.

Center Tab: Text is centred as it is typed at the tab stop as in the example below:

| Dog | Horse | Snake |
| Camel | Kangaroo | Elephant |

Right Tab: Text is aligned on the right as in the example below:

| Black | White | Red |
| Auburn | Turquoise | Strawberry |

Decimal Tab: Text before the decimal point extends to the left — the decimal points align with each other; text after the decimal point extends to the right as in the example below:

| 12.458 | 289.67 | 1.23 |
| 5,678.890 | 2.78 | 1,234.98 |

2. Leader Characters

The Leader Character is a solid, dotted, or dashed line that fills the space used by a tab character, thus drawing the reader's eye across the line from the data on the left to the data on the right as in the example below:

Portugal .... 8 points
Ireland .... 12 points

WORD PROCESSING — LEVEL 2

Practical Assignment 3

1. Create the following documents for merging.

1. Save under the appropriate filenames.

1. Print one copy of each letter on A4 paper.

<u>30 Marks</u>

ASSIGNMENT 3

VARIABLES

<u>Letter 1</u>

Mr Pat Hurley of Sea Breeze, Rosscarbery, Co. Cork, enquired on 25 August 1994, about CPU Holders. John Roche informed him by letter on 2 September that it would take at least 10 days from receipt of order to deliver required goods.

<u>Letter 2</u>

Mr Roche wrote to Ms Rita Byrne of Castlewhite, Bandon, Co. Cork, on 5 December 1994, in response to her query on 28 November 1994, regarding Secretarial Workstations. It will take 21 days from receipt of order before a delivery can be made.

<u>Letter 3</u>

Mr Barry Condon of Main St, Mallow, Co. Cork, asked Mr Roche on 28 September 1994 about the possibility of purchasing Computer Tables. Mr Roche replied on 7 October 1994, enclosing a catalogue and reminding Mr Condon that it would take 28 days from receipt of an order for the goods to be delivered.

<u>Letter 4</u>

Mr John Shine of Perceival Square, Kanturk, Co. Cork, rang Mr Roche on 20 March 1994, to see if he had wooden tables in stock. Mr Roche gave him the information he wanted on 17 April 1994, and also informed Mr Shine that, regardless of the urgency, all orders take 25 days from receipt of order before delivery could be made.

TASK 7A

- Use the decimal tab settings for the following exercise — the left column will be keyed in at the margin.
- Use single-line spacing on A5 landscape paper.
- Save as 'Hickinson MW'.

HICKINSON & CO LTD ← *bold*

Report for years ended:1989-1993

Year to 31 March	1989	1990	1992	1993
Group profit before tax	345.67	344.67	321.23	673.45
Taxation	565.67	456.78	567.89	326.78
Group net profit	235.67	456.78	567.89	765.67
Revenue reserves	246.78	897.98	765.65	653.32

Practical Assignment 2

1. Display this table attractively, centre vertically and horizontally.

2. Save your document under the filename 'Gifts03' for printing out later, as per your teacher's instructions.

<u>25 Marks</u>

(Re-arrange in date order)

(Caps, Centre, Bold & U/s)

Farewell Gifts

Resigned on	Staff Member	Position	Gift	Cost
25 June 1993	Michael Tobin	Vice-Chairman	Holiday Voucher	2,500
27 May 1993	John Walsh	Executive Officer	Colour TV	£ 300
14 July 1993	Marcella Hogan	Typist	Tea Service	£ 120
21 January 1993	Rita Moore	Personnel Assistant	Silver Pen	£ 85
12 August 1993	Denis O'Connell	Clerical Officer	Prize Bonds	£ 150

2 All staff had more than 10 years service

1 All staff had been exemplary members of staff. WORK FORCE

(Rule)

TASK 7B

- Create the following document using the decimal tab.
- Use single-line spacing and print once on A4 landscape paper.
- Save as 'Bambury MW'.

BED SUPERSTORES USAGE			
Acton	56.78	76.99	99.56
Aylesbury	998.78	232.32	123.45
Bambury	4324.42	324.44	234.89
Christchurch	4234.34	432.32	43.34
Isle of Wight	534.45	2343.23	2433.43

Rarities and Errors

One of the rarest stamps in the world is the British Guiana 1-cent issue of 1856 printed in black on magenta-coloured paper. A school-boy in the colony found it in 1873, and sold it to a local collector for 6s. In 1922, it was sold for £7,343.

Two very rare stamps are the Mauritius penny and the two penny of 1847. These were designed and printed locally.

Paper, Gum and Perforation

The paper or stamps is made form pulp contianing rags and esparto grass as well as wood. These yield a cellulose with very strong fibres so that the paper obtained is tough and flexible. Stamp Club.   *N P*

Over 500 towns in Great Britain have a club or society for stamp collectors. these clubs hold meetings every week or so at which talks are given, collections are exhibited and duplicates are exchanged every week or so, ~~at which talks are given, collections are exhibited and duplicates are exchanged~~.

How Stamps are Made   *needed*

When a new postage stamp is ~~required~~, the government may hold a competition to see which artist can produce the best design. These companies have their own designers, who are not only skilled artists but have a complete understanding of the processes through which a design must pass be fore it apepars as a finished stamp.

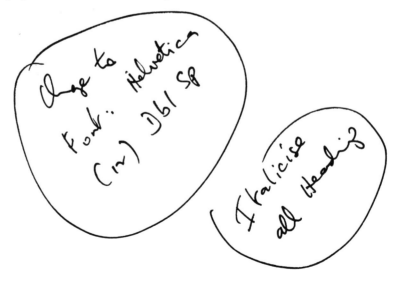

Chnge to Helvetica font: (rn) Dbl SP

Italicise all Headings

TASK 7C

- Create the following document using the decimal tab.
- Use single-line spacing and print once on A4 landscape paper.
- Save as 'Haughton MW'.

W HAUGHTON PLC — *bold*

STATE OF ACCOUNTS — *Italics*

Year Ending, 31 December — u/s

Rule

	1992	1993	1994
Deferred Taxation	234,072.00	123,876.09	234,567.99
Reserves	8,900.00	345,987.00	234,567.00
Quoted Investments	234,567.89	234,568.09	356,789.00
Net Current Assets	345,678.90	212,345.00	345,678.00
Current Liabilities	56,789.00	32,457.00	21,347.43

bold →

SAMPLE III

WORD PROCESSING — LEVEL 2

Practical Assignment 1

1. Key in the document below; proofread, correct where necessary and make the changes as indicated.

2. Please use 1" (2.5 cm) for the left and right margins.

3. Ragged or justified line endings are acceptable.

4. Insert text under 'Rarities' and indent 2" from the margin in order to leave space for the picture to be attached.

5. Save your document under the filename 'Stamps02' for printing out later, as per your teacher's instructions.

<u>25 Marks</u>

Centre & u/s

STAMPS AND STAMP COLLECTING *leave 1 clear line*
The collecting of postage stamps (sometimes called "philately"), is a popular hobby and although most girls lose interest in it ~~and although most girls lose interest in it~~ as they grow older, many boys go on collecting.

Postage stamps, in the form of printed sticky labels that could be bought at the post office and labels that could be bought at the and fixed to letters to pay for carrying them, were first introudcedin Great Britain. The *N P* first stamps, which showed the had of Queen Victoria, were apenny black one and a twopenny blue one. They did not carry the name of the coutnry as that was unnecessary for no other nation then used stamps. *ever since,* This practicehas been continued with the stamps of Great Britain The stamps were first put on sale to the public on May 1, 1840, although their use was not alloweduntil May 6. They were printed in sheets of 240 from which which they had to be cut by scissors.

<u>How to Collect Stamps</u> *beginner*
The best way for a starterto begin a stamp collection is to buy a packet of 500 or 1,000 mixed stamps. Such a jacket bought from a reliable stamp-shop contain stamps, but they are clean and in good condition and with hardly any duplicates among them. *only common*
Once this start has been made, it is not difficult to add tothe colelction. *uc* relatives and holidays can be a great help. So can some office workers, as many offices receiveaquantity of letters from abroad, and often the stamps are thrown away with the envelopes. Another excellent way of obtaining stamps is by swopping duplicates with other collectors
Specialisation

Most beginners collect everything and there is much to be saidfor this. It teaches the ways about the stamp world and through the pages of the catalogue, and in this manner the new collector obtains a lot of useful general knowledge. However, after some time he or she usually begins to be more interested in the stamps of one country than another. it is, of *uc* course, quite possible to be interested in the stamps of several countries. Generally speaking, however, it is too much to expect anyone to be able to go on collecting the stamps of all countries — *there are just too many of them.*

TASK 7D

- Create the following document using the decimal tab.
- Use double-line spacing.
- Save as 'Tariff MW'.
- Print one copy on A4 landscape paper.

Tariff Sheet

Conference Accommodation

Warner House	125.50	2,160.00
Sea Crest	630.00	1,200.00
Adler House	1,230.00	200.00
Green Crescent	28.50	180.00
Guttland View	35.00 (³45.00)	165.50
Old Mill House	1,440.00	195.00
Trafalgar House Lodge	555.00	2,350.00
Palace Lodge	42.00	270.00
Royal Hotel	45.00	300.00
Clifton ~~Green~~ Hotel View	35.00	210.00

(Note: Sea Crest and Warner House second-column values are transposed by arrows — 2,160.00 / 1,200.00)

(Rule)

Practical Assignment 3

1. Create the following documents for merging.

2. Save under the appropriate filenames.

3. Print one copy of each letter on A4 paper.

<u>30 Marks</u>

Assignment 3 Variables

<u>Letter 1</u>

Mr John Fox of Main St, Ballydehob, Co Cork, was talking to Mr James Murphy yesterday (24 April, 1995). In this letter now, Mr Murphy wants to inform Mr Fox that Tile King's tiler, Mr Brian Carlton, will come to assess the job on Monday, 12 May.

<u>Letter 2</u>

Mr Murphy wrote to Mr Michael Phelan of Sea View, Schull, Co Cork, on 16 May, 1994. He had been speaking to Mr Phelan the previous Wednesday and he now wanted to let him know that his tiler, Mr John Moore, would come to Mr Phelan's house, as promised, on Monday, 24 June.

<u>Letter 3</u>

Further to a conversation the previous week, Mr Larry Kingston of Baker's Row, Youghal, Co Cork, was written to on 24 August, 1994, to inform him that Mr John Nyhan, the tiler, would come to give an assessment on the proposed work on Monday, 6 September.

TASK 7E

- Create the following document using the decimal tab.
- Use single-line spacing and print one copy on A4 landscape paper.
- Save as 'Revenue MW'.

$	$	$	(Rule)
2,345.60	4,567.80	2,567.00	
5,677.99	52,123.90	882,123.90	
1,400.50	2,456.90	2,345.90	
8,900.90	125,678.00	223,456.00	
3,456.00	3,456.99	3,488.90 76	

1. Display this table attractively, centre vertically and horizontally.

2. Save your document under the filename 'IIT01' for printing out later, as per your teacher's instructions.

<u>25 Marks</u>

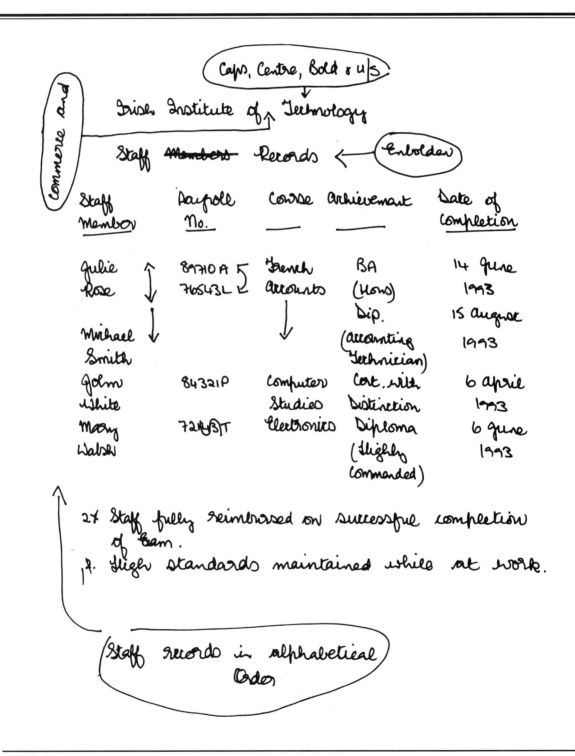

TASK 7F

- Create the following document using the center tab.
- Use single-line spacing and print one copy on A4 landscape paper.
- Save as 'Beamish MW'.

Beamish MSL Results			
Cobh Wanderers	St Mary's	Midleton	Rockmount
Avondale United	Douglas Hall	Carrigaline	Youghal
College Corinthians	Cobh Ramblers	Avondale	Tramore Athletic

The Morse Code

Most other systems of signalling use the code invented by the American, Samuel Morse. In the Morse code each letter and figure is represented by a different group of long and shorts. For example, B is a long and three shorts and M is two long.

~~The Electric Telegraph~~

(In 1837,) Charles Wheatstone and William F. Cooke set up an electric telegraph linking Euston railway station in London with the station at Camden Town about a mile away. Their early instruments took the form of magnetic needles which were deflected by sending an electric current through a coil of wire surrounding the needle.

Radio, or wireless telegraphy as it was called in the beginning, began with the theory of the Scottish scientist James Clerk Maxwell. He showed that it ~~smut~~ MUST be possible to create electromagnetic waves that would travel through space at the speed of light. His theory was confirmed by a German scientist and methods of producing and receiving the electromagnetic waves were developed towards the end of the 19 century by an Italian.

The ability to send messages over great ~~over great~~ distances ~~with the need for wires~~ brought about a revolution in signalling. Before wireless telegraphy, a ship owner wishing to send a message to one of his ships at sea generally had to wait until the ship reached its next prot.

In the same way, warships sent reports once they were out of sight of land. ~~Wireless telegraphy changed all this.~~ Wireless telegraphy changed all this. For ~~example,~~ it makes possible radio telephone conversation with ships at sea. ~~For example, it makes possible radio telephone conversation with ships at sea.~~

uc

Change to Indented style, font: Arial (10) 1½ line sp

TASK 7G

- Create the following document using the center tab.
- Use single-line spacing and print one copy on A4 landscape paper.
- Save as 'Calculators MW'.

<u>CALCULATORS</u>

Main Brands Only

Features	H Citizen CX75	I Sharp+	J Casio+ HR150L	K Casio HR150L
Digits displayed	10	12	10	10
Printer speed lines	1.7	1.2	1.8	1.6
Memories	4 key	4 key		
Time calculations			*	
Independent memory %		*		*
Key				
Change sign (+/-)				
Fixed decimals	*		*	
Sub total	*		*	
Item count	*	*	*	*
Mark up/mark down	*	*	*	*
Floating/fixed	*	*	*	*
decimal point		*	*	
	*		*	
Decimal cut off	*	*	*	
		*		
Power source	Battery/Mains	Battery/Mains	4xA4/Mains	4xA4/Mains
Ink/roller ribbon	Roller	Roller	Roller	Roller
Paper roll width (mm)	58	58	58	58
Size (mm)	160x40x210	151x204x51	162x214x51	162x214x51
Product Code	178658	260229	290422	290414

+Optional adaptor required for mains supply

WORD PROCESSING — LEVEL 2

Practical Assignment 1

1. Key in the document below; proofread, correct where necessary and make the changes as indicated.

2. Please use 1" (2.5 cm) for the left and right margins.

3. Ragged or justified line endings are acceptable.

4. Insert text under 'Morse Code' and indent 2" from the margin in order to leave space for the graphic to be attached at a later time.

5. Save your document under the filename 'Signal01' for printing out later, as per your teacher's instructions.

<u>25 Marks</u>

Centre, embolden & u/s

SIGNALLING

method

Signalling is a ~~means~~ of communication, which is the sending of information . In signalling, however, the information is passed by signs instead of by speaking directly to the other person or by sending him a written message. [In the simpler forms of signalling, the signs used are those that can be either directly seen or heard.   *N P*

Signals can be:

Semaphore Signals

In the Napoleonic Wars two "telegraph" systems as they were called, were used forlong-distance signalling on land. The British system had a fixed frame ~~had a fixed frame~~ showing six spaceseach of which was occupied by an octagonal plate.   *∧ #*

Each plate was pivoted so that it could be turned either to fill the space or leave it empty. Withthis system, 64 different signals could be sent, and a chain of these these stations were set up between London and Portsmouth.

<u>Flag Signals</u>   *(hundreds of)*

Flags have been used for signals between ships foryears. The earliest known code of signals was drawn up in the 9 century by the Emperor Leo VI, but the first recorded use recorded use of a signal at sea was in the year, 1337.

TASK 7H

- Create the following document using the right tab.
- Use single-line spacing and print one copy on A4 landscape paper.
- Save as 'Markets MW'.

FINANCIAL MARKETS			
China	Hong Kong	India	Indonesia
Malaysia	Philippines	Singapore	South Korea
Taiwan	Thailand	Argentina	Brazil
Chile	Colombia	Mexico	Venezuela
Egypt	Greece	Israel	South Africa
Turkey	Czech Republic	Hungary	Poland

Letter 1

[1]   Today's date
[2]   Ms Mary Moore
        Sea View
        CLOYNE
        Co Cork
[3]   Ms Moore
[4]   Stillorgan
[5]   Clients
[6]   Saturday, 12 February, 1995.

Letter 2

[1]   Today's date
[2]   Mr Matt Walsh
        Templemartin
        DUNGOURNEY
        Co Cork
[3]   Mr Walsh
[4]   Dundrum
[5]   Customers
[6]   Monday, 18 March, 1995.

Letter 3

[1]   Today's date
[2]   Mr John Collins
        Moore Street
        FERMOY
        Co Cork
[3]   Mr Collins
[4]   last week
[5]   Rathfarnham
[6]   Monday, 4 April, 1995.

TASK 71

- Create the following document using the right tab.
- Use single-line spacing and print one copy on A4 landscape paper.
- Save as 'Services MW'.

CLASSIFICATION OF SERVICES — Spaced Caps

Entertainment	Sales and Exchanges	Holidays
Theatres	Television	Chalets
Cabaret	Tape Recorders	Caravans
Clubs	Radios	Accommodation
Cinemas	Stables	Flats
Pool	Weights	Hostels
Sailing	Racquets	Hotels
Walking	Media	Tents
Riding	Bikes	Camps

All columns are right-aligned

Practical Assignment 3

1. Key in the following draft letter taking care to insert the symbols for the variables exactly as shown.

2. Save your document under the filename 'Hols01' for printing out later, as per your teacher's instructions.

3. Create three separate letters with the variables given; save each one for printing out later.

<u>30 Marks</u>

---

[1]

[2]

Dear [3]

Holiday Brochure : 1995 *(Underline and centre)*

As you may be aware, we have opened a new branch at [4]. [To ~~cele~~ celebrate this *(CELEBRATE)* expansion in business, we are offering our regular [5], 20% off any holiday booked before [6].   NP

We enclose our current brochure and look forward to doing business with you in 1995.

Yours —
SUNSHINE HOLIDAYS

Jim Ryan

TASK 7J

- Create the following document using the right tab.
- Use single-line spacing and print one copy on A4 landscape paper.
- Save as 'Services MW'.

BROCHURE COLLECTION			
People Products	New Furniture	Conservatory Blinds	Gemstones
Clothing Co	Stoves Range Cookers	Fitting Shoes	Sinks of Note
Garage Doors	Leisure Breaks	Leisure Times	House Interiors
Laminated Flooring	Painted Floorboards	Photographs	Chequeboard
Garden Shades	Plant Finder	Flower Power	Plant Food
Brilliant Blooms	Reader Garden	Conservatory	Garden Range
Fine Carpets	Oriental Styles	Mixer Paints	Shower Doors

WORD PROCESSING — LEVEL 2

Practical Assignment 2

1. Display this table attractively, centre vertically and horizontally.

2. Save your document under the filename 'Office02' for printing out later, as per your teacher's instructions.

<u>25 Marks</u>

Office Furniture *(CAPS, CENTRE, BOLD & U/S)*

Description	Model	No. *(IN FULL)*	Value	Years Old
Bookcases (Solid Oak)	HB 987A	3	£1750	30
Executive Chairs	CH 9743B	6	£540	3
Filing Cabinets (all 4-Drawer)	JK 7532P	4	£600	5
Storage Unit	SP53 IT	6	£1,200	8
Curved Desks	DP 5214S	8	£3,500	6

ARTWORK ON A SEPARATE PAGE

1. Curved Desks' edges are protected by 2.8mm solid wood lippin' *(LIPPIN)*

2. Bookcases are complete with two shelves and clear glass doors fixed with 90° hinges.

Place in value order — most valuable first

Speed Training

Day 1

Warm-Up

Type each word or phrase **three times in sequence** example: **add add add**

add	dad	ads	as	fad	gag	gas	sad
had	has	all	lad	lass	ask	flask	shall
sag	jag	lag	flag	saga	flak	dash	lash
gash	glad	slash	salsa	salad	dallas	alaska	fall

deed	deer	dear	feed	feet	rear	east	else
food	foot	good	root	hood	idea	idle	gala
this	that	with	week	kite	keep	kiss	jeep
peep	peel	pass	page	pair	pale	peak	pear

fleet	glass	fight	right	sight	tight	light	slight
why	white	who	these	those	utter	upset	upper
jelly	jolly	yeast	youth	quart	queue	quiet	quit
quilt	quote	float	flood	waste	what	shout	loud

as glad as dad;	as sad as dad;	a lass asks a lad;	a lass has a fag;
she is proud;	you like the sea;	we had a wish;	take a seat;

Now, Time Yourself

Type the following words **ONLY ONCE** and see how many you can do in one minute
(in case you finish all four lines ahead of time start again):

lass	flag	saga	flak	dash	lash	gash	glad	fall	9 wpm
deed	feed	feet	deer	dear	rear	east	else	gala	18 wpm
food	foot	good	root	hood	idea	idle	this	that	27 wpm
with	week	kite	keep	kiss	jeep	peep	peel	pass	36 wpm

Speed Training

Day 2

Warm-Up

Type each word **three times in sequence** example: **set set set**

One-Hand Words for the Left Hand

set	few	see	get	are	was	at	as	we	be
a	best	date	case	fact	area	free	rate	were	car
act	war	tax	ever	card	face				

One-Hand Words for the Right Hand

my	up	no	on	only	you	upon	nun	moon	noon
lull	noun	nylon	poll	polo	pomp	pompom	pool	poppy	pull
pulp	pump	pun							

Double-Letter Words

well	good	need	feel	look	less	call	been	will	off
too	see	all	book	bill	tell	still	small	too	free
soon	week	room	took	keep					

Balance-Hand Words

us	so	do	me	am	go	the	and	for	but
of	to	is	it	he	by	or	an	if	due
pay	got	big	air	with	they	when	end	own	man
then	work	both	down	form	city	their	them	than	also
such	make	hand	paid	held	half	this	world	field	name

Now, Time Yourself

Type the following words **ONLY ONCE** and see how many you can do in one minute (in case you finish all four lines ahead of time start again):

best	date	case	fact	area	free	rate	were	card	9 wpm
face	only	upon	moon	noon	lull	noun	poll	polo	18 wpm
pool	pull	pulp	pump	well	good	need	feel	look	27 wpm
less	call	been	will	book	bill	tell	still	soon	36 wpm

Speed Training

Day 3

Warm-Up

Type each word **three times in sequence** example: **soon soon soon**

soon	seat	wish	like	they	deep	root
then	when	with	keep	took	room	week

thin	then	city	form	down	both	work
half	held	paid	hand	make	such	also

mill	bill	fill	pill	fame	name	tame
tall	call	mall	wall	mate	date	taste

zeal	zest	zero	zips	zebra
lax	wax	fox	box	fix

call	cake	city	cool	class
vase	veil	vest	very	vote
ball	book	bike	bird	bear

noon	nose	nice	near	neat
mail	mess	meet	mild	mood

Now, Time Yourself

Type the following words **ONLY ONCE** and see how many you can do in one minute
(in case you finish all four lines ahead of time start again):

room	root	soon	mood	noon	book	took	cool	work	9 wpm
fill	pill	bill	mill	nice	mild	zips	like	with	18 wpm
ball	mall	tall	wall	call	fall	held	half	veil	27 wpm
mate	date	fame	tame	name	when	then	than	thin	36 wpm

43

Speed Training

Day 4

Warm-Up

Type each word **three times in sequence** example: **mood mood mood**

mood	mild	name	near	bird	bike	veil	vase
cool	cake	zero	zest	meet	make	mail	noon
nose	dose	rose	city	pity	male	pale	rail
meet	meat	read	lead	nice	dice	rice	mice

I	you	he	she	it	we	you	they
my	your	his	her	its	our	their	to
in	on	at	of	if	or	and	but
this	that	these	those	there	through	no	yes

what	who	where	why	whose	whom	which	when
about	above	under	near	between	over	beside	beyond

eat	drink	sleep	wash	cry	fly	laugh	write
read	play	stay	sit	stand	dance	walk	run
climb	jump	drive	push	sell	buy	swim	dive

Now, Time Yourself

Type the following words **ONLY ONCE** and see how many you can do in one minute
(in case you finish all four lines ahead of time start again):

this	that	what	whom	near	wash	read	play	stay	9 wpm
walk	jump	push	sell	dive	your	they	rice	mice	18 wpm
rail	pale	male	pity	city	rose	dose	lead	veil	27 wpm
vase	name	mild	mood	moon	zero	zest	cool	cake	36 wpm

45

Speed Training

Day 5

Warm-Up

Type each word or sentence **three times in sequence** example: **east east east**

east	west	north	south	up	down	in	out
one	two	three	four	five	six	seven	eight
nine	ten	eleven	twelve	thirteen	fourteen	fifteen	twenty
white	black	grey	red	purple	green	yellow	orange
pink	brown	blue	gold	silver			

father	mother	uncle	aunt	brother	sister	son	daughter
come	go	throw	catch	watch	sing	talk	walk
kick	listen	think	roar	dig	water	point	look
find	give	cut	cook	open	close	take	teach
break	milk	home					

I like bananas.	You went home.	He eats an apple a day.	She cut the grass.
We talk a lot.	Dinner is ready.		

Father is happy.	Mother opened the door.	Roses are red.
Milk is white.	Apples are red, green or yellow.	

Now, Time Yourself

Type the following words **ONLY ONCE** and see how many you can do in one minute (in case you finish all four lines ahead of time start again):

east	west	down	four	five	nine	grey	pink	blue	9 wpm
gold	milk	home	aunt	come	sing	talk	kick	roar	18 wpm
look	find	give	cook	open	take	like	cake	door	27 wpm
pill	bill	wall	call	tall	them	than	such	also	36 wpm

Speed Training

Day 6

Warm-Up

Type each word or expression **three times in sequence** example: **about about about**

A	about	above	after	ahead	alive
B	beach	begin	bingo	broad	build
C	cheer	cargo	cover	check	clock
D	daily	dress	diary	ditch	dizzy

E	eager	eight	elect	enjoy	enter
F	fable	fetch	first	flair	forty
G	globe	grade	grant	great	guest
H	hello	heart	honey	horse	house

I	ideal	input	issue	ivory	inlet
J	jeans	jewel	joint	judge	jelly
K	khaki	kinky	kitty	knock	knack
L	label	lasso	learn	lemon	light

about me,	above all,	after eight,	at the beach,
begin now,	cover it up,	check it out,	build up,
daily mail,	dress code,	diary notes,	elect him,
enjoy it,	enter now,	first class,	great taste,
guest house,	good guess,		

Now, Time Yourself

Type the following words **ONLY ONCE** and see how many you can do in one minute
(in case you finish all four lines ahead of time start again):

alive	above	beach	bingo	check	cheer	dress	9 wpm
dizzy	enter	enjoy	first	forty	great	guest	18 wpm
hello	heart	ideal	issue	jeans	jelly	knock	28 wpm
knack	learn	lemon	after	ahead	cargo	cover	37 wpm

Speed Training
Day 7

Warm-Up

Type each word or expression **three times in sequence** example: **madam madam madam**

M	madam	magic	match	medal	merry
N	night	noble	novel	nurse	never
O	onion	opera	orbit	order	organ
P	paint	paper	pasta	phone	piano

Q	quake	quote	quick	quiet	quite
R	radio	ready	refer	right	river
S	salad	sandy	scale	scene	screw
T	table	teens	thank	think	toast

U	under	union	unite	until	upper
V	value	villa	visit	vital	vocal
W	water	weird	whale	wheel	white
Y	yacht	yeast	youth	yield	yours
Z	zebra	zippy	zonal	zooms	zones

the magic key	noble reasons	never again	onion chips
opera house	in orbit	paint brush	pasta sauce
phone book	piano player	quick decision	quiet move
radio speaker	ready to go	refer to	right away
salad bar	sandy beaches		

Now, Time Yourself

Type the following words **ONLY ONCE** and see how many you can do in one minute
(in case you finish all four lines ahead of time start again):

merry	medal	nurse	never	opera	orbit	paint	piano	9 wpm
pasta	quick	quiet	radio	ready	salad	sandy	scene	18 wpm
table	toast	under	until	visit	villa	water	whale	28 wpm
white	youth	toast	zebra	zones	magic	match	novel	37 wpm

Speed Training

Day 8

Warm-Up

Type each word or phrase **three times in sequence** example: **fable fable fable**

fable	table	stable	cable	sable
rent	tent	lent	sent	bent

night	right	fight	light	sight
dough	rough	cough	tough	laugh

agree	disagree	cover	discover
care	careful	cheer	cheerful

safe	unsafe	happy	unhappy
prove	improve	polite	impolite

neat	neatness	sweet	sweetness
action	lotion	caution	definition

in a fable	on the table	in our stable	with a cable
pay the rent	buy a tent	never sent	totally bent

last night	alright	a big fight	out of sight
a tough cough	a big laugh	a rough guy	a sweet tooth

Now, Time Yourself

Type the following words **ONLY ONCE** and see how many you can do in one minute
(in case you finish all four lines ahead of time start again):

cable	stable	rent	tent	fight	light	rough	9 wpm
cough	tough	lent	bent	sight	night	laugh	19 wpm
draft	cover	play	form	prove	close	alike	29 wpm
sweet	right	neat	help	tooth	fable	table	39 wpm

Speed Training

Day 9

Warm-Up

Type each word, expression or sentence **three times in sequence**
example: **guest house guest house guest house**

guest house	great table	elect her	enjoy it
daily mail	dress code	check in	begin now

after eight	above all	first class	build up
noble reasons	never again	refer to	right away

salad bar	sandy beaches	radio speaker	in orbit
onion chips	opera house	phone book	paint brush

until now	upper class	put aside	off white
table tennis	rye toast	on the scene	screw driver

kinky curls	knock out	jelly beans	never judge
fetch it	forty something	cargo ship	bingo hall

Now, Time Yourself

Type the following words **ONLY ONCE** and see how many you can do in one minute
(in case you finish all four lines ahead of time start again):

guest house	dress code	check in	first class	9 wpm
never again	right away	sandy beaches	onion chips	18 wpm
phone book	kinky curls	table tennis	jelly beans	27 wpm
cargo ship	daily mail	until now	under offer	36 wpm

Speed Training

Day 10

Warm-Up

Type each word or sentence **three times in sequence** example: **Anne Anne Anne**

Anne	Jack	Jill	Peter	Mary	Laura	Paul	Steve
John	Tony	London	Dublin	Bristol	Leeds	York	Kent
Dorset	Devon	Surrey	Essex				

England	Wales	Scotland	Northern Ireland		Greece	France	Spain
Great Britain		Europe	America	Africa	Asia	Antarctica	

Monday	Tuesday	Wednesday	Thursday	Friday	Saturday	Sunday	New Year

January	February	March	April	May	June	July	August
September	October	November	December				

Jack and Jill have a guest house.
Laura and Paul went to the salad bar.
Mary and Tony love white sandy beaches.
Anne and Steve looked in the phone book.

Now, Time Yourself

Type the following words **ONLY ONCE** and see how many you can do in one minute (in case you finish all four lines ahead of time start again):

John	Jack	Jill	Paul	Tony	Anne	Mary	Laura	9 wpm
Wales	Leeds	Kent	Asia	June	July	April	May	19 wpm
Europe	Africa	France	Greece	Surrey	Dorset			29 wpm
London	Dublin	Monday	Sunday	Friday	August			39 wpm

GUIDELINES FOR CREATING A MAIL MERGE DOCUMENT

1. Click on **Tools** and from menu click on Mail Merge.

2. Click on No 1 Create and then Form Letters then Active Window.

3. Click on No 2 Get Data and Create Data Source.

4. Delete Field Name you <u>don't</u> want and add Field Names you do want

    to use in you Data Source. Click OK.

5. **Save**

6. Click on Edit Data Source.

7. Key in Records in Data Form. Click Add New. Repeat for 2nd

    Record.

8. When complete click on OK.

9. Create your letter by clicking on 'Insert Merge Field' making sure

    your cursor is in the right position.

    Insert Ref and continue inserting data in same way then type your

    letter. **Save**

10 Click ~~on Tools~~ and then Mail Merge. ON TOOL BAR

11 Merge all Records to a New Document Click on Merge.

12 New Letters created. **Save**

TASK 7K

- Create the following document using the right tab for the first two columns; the left tab for the third and the decimal tab for the fourth and fifth.
- Use single-line spacing and print one copy on A4 landscape paper.
- Save as 'Signmaker MW'.

19mm	10m	2300 Signmaker	£2,450.00	£2,456.00
12mm	2mm	1535/123 Tapewriter	£12,345.60	£14,345.68
9 mm	3mm	1845 Labelmaker	£12,456.70	£14,560.00
12mm	5mm	1765 Tapewriter	£2,567.89	£3,245.60
13 mm	5mm	4578 Tapewriter	£2,456.70	£4,567.90

Milky Way

If these theories, or something like them turn out to be right, then very many stars may have globes going around them. There could be as many as 100,000,000 planetary systems altogether within the Milky Way alone, and many of these could have globes like those in our own solar system.

leave 1 clear line

Mercury

Mercury, (is nearest to the Sun, and goes round it in the longest time. Mercury turns once on its axis every 59 days. It spins several times in the time that it takes to travel twice around the Sun.

the smaller planets

Globes:

Facts about the globes are well known are well known:

Venus

The planet, Venus isslightly smaller than the Earth, and moves around the sun in less time. *after the sun and moon, it can be the brightest object in the sky.*

leave 1 clear line

Jupiter

Jupiter is the giant of the is the giant of the solar system, more than three times as massive as its nearest rival, Saturn, and over 300 times as massive as our Earth. When favourably placed, Jupiter is one of the brightest objects in the sky. *#*

Saturn

Saturn, the sixth planet, is in many ways, themost remarkable of all. It is circled by a system of circles, which, when viewed though a telescope is the most striking and beautiful of all the globes.

The Asteroids

Between Mars and Jupiter, which is the fifth planet form the Sun, lie the orbits of theminor globes, or asteroids. The first asteroid was discovered on January 1, 1801, by the Italian astronomer, Giueseppe Piazzi. He *created* it *Ceres after the Roman goddess of* *CALLED* *agriculture.*

Change to Indented style – One bse sp.

change font to Courier (12)

TASK 7L

- Create the following document using the right tab. Set up leader dots for the second column.

- Use single-line spacing and print one copy on A4 landscape paper.

- Save as 'Williams MW'.

Williams and Ball Limited
Statement of Source and Application of Funds ← Bold
for the year ended 31 March 1982

	£	£
	£000	£000
	11981	1982

Source of Funds

Profit revenue account	6,079	5,878
Adjustment for items not involving the movement of funds:		
Depreciation and amortisation	60	61
Share of profit of associated company	(39)	(4)
	6,100	5,935
Sale of Investment and other properties	1910	2,544
Issue of shares	112	116
Issue of Loan stock, net of expenses	21,477	—
	29,599	8,595

NCVA — Word Processing Practical

Pupils preparing for this examination may benefit from doing the following exercises (prepared by the author) which are similar in design to past NCVA exams.

SAMPLE I

WORD PROCESSING — LEVEL 2

Practical Assignment 1

1. Key in the document below; proofread, correct and make the changes as indicated.

2. Please use 1" (2.5 cm) for left and right margins.

3. Ragged or justified line endings are accepted.

4. Insert text under paragraph 5 'Milky Way' and indent 2" from the margin in order to leave space for the picture to be attached later.

5. Save your document under the filename 'Solar01' for printing out later, as per your teacher's instructions.

25 Marks

SOLAR SYSTEM — *Bld, Spaced Caps, Centre & u/s*

the Globes

Astronomers are not certain how the the Sun, and the rest of the solar system came into existence. There are ~~various suggestions~~, but none is entirely satisfactory. *suggested explanations*

This problem is very difficult, because knowledge of different sciences - mathematics, physics, as well as astronomy - is needed by scientists by scientists who ~~analyse~~ it. *study*

20th Century

According to the explanation favoured at the middle of the twentieth century, the Sun and globes were formed at roughly the same time, out of out of an enormous, slowly turning cloud of gases and cool dust Part of the cloud collapsed, over a period of several million years, to form the Sun.

18th Century

Astronomers are still truing to wrok out the details the details of this theory. It may turn out that some of the details are wrong, but the general idea has been around ~~has been around~~ since the late 18th century and has a good chance of beingwong.

TASK 7M

- Create the following document using the right tab. Set up leader dots for the second column.
- Use double-line spacing and print one copy on A4 landscape paper.
- Save as 'Huston MW'.

Huston Word and Data Processing Ltd — Bold

Sales for Period Ending: June 1994

Type	Cork	Dublin	Galway	Tuam
Sony Disks	213,897	4,567	2,142	1.897
Pelltech	89,567	3,6234	3,278	657
Verbatim	£234,5(83)	4,567	5,455	5(67)3
Rexel Diskettes	789	5,456	5,444	980
Guides Classic	790	4,345	3,456	532
Sasco Cartridges	234,567	4,567	3,456	3,234

Guidelines

This Unit concentrates on exercises which should help prepare the student for the Word Processing Practical — Level 2, which is set by the Department of Education under the National Council for Vocational Awards (NCVA).

TASK 7N

- Create the following document using the right tab. Set up leader dots for the second column.

- Use single-line spacing and print one copy on A4 landscape paper.

- Save as 'Associated MW'.

Application of Funds

Additions to investments and other properties	11,562	13,061
Additions to other fixed assets, net of disposals	74	74
Increase in stock of trading properties	2,302	314
Other capital payments	34	358
Loan to associated company	38	77
Taxation	1,379	1,120
Dividends	1,803	1,561
Net Increase in working capital	834	1,991
	18,021	18,556
	11,578	(9,961)

Decrease (Increase) in Borrowings

Long Term	8,897	(6,437)
Short Term	2,681	(3,524)
	11,578	(9,961)

Unit 14

NATIONAL COUNCIL FOR VOCATIONAL AWARDS

(NCVA)

Sample Papers

TASK 70

- Create the following document using the decimal tab. Set up leader dots for the first column.
- Use single-line spacing and print one copy on A4 landscape paper.
- Save as 'Wilson's MW'.

Wilsons Scaffolding for Sub-Station [BOLD]

Diablo 4.06	£ 25.50	£ 44.75	£ 56.45	£ 66.44
Quieme 6.80	£ 45.00	£ 65.87	£ 77.50	£ 85.50
Ricoh 5.80	£ 65.70	£ 75.40	£ 86.50	£ 92.50
Panaoi 10.45	£ 101.35	£ 450.89	£ 453.45	£ 560.50
Rexiel 24.89	£ 234.00	£ 1,450.32	£ 1,345.50	£ 16,900.00
Aecoi 56.90	£ 2,345.00	£ 2,654.00	£ 4,560.00	£ 21,900.00

Variables

Booking 1:

Mr John Walsh of 4 O'Brien's Tce, Macroom, Co Cork, wants to reserve a Mobile Home with 4 beds from Saturday, 30 June, 1995, to Saturday, 14 July, 1995.

He doesn't require Bedrooms En-Suite. However, he wants to be supplied with a TV and to have a Swimming Pool on Site and to be near the beach. He doesn't want to avail of Baby-sitting Service or Room Service. He will not need to use a Telephone or the Garden during his stay. Majorca is his first preference. He will do his own cleaning.

Booking 2:

Ms Kate O'Connell of 45 Sligo St, Cork, is interested in staying in a Villa in Benidorm with a Swimming Pool near the Beach, with her family from 12 July, 1995, to 27 July, 1995. Her party need the use of five beds with 2 Bedrooms En-Suite. They don't need Room or Cleaning Service or the use of a Telephone. They will require the services of a Baby-Sitter. They are very keen, also, to have the use of the garden.

Booking 3:

John O'Brien of King St, Navan, Co Meath, wants to book a Chalet in Rimini with a Swimming Pool near the Beach, for his family from 23 July, 1995, to 7 August, 1995. The Chalet must have 6 Beds. Bedrooms En-Suite are not required. He will need to reserve a Baby-sitter during his stay but he is not interested in any of the other facilities/services such as: Garden, Telephone, TV, Room or Cleaning Service.

Booking 4:

Killian Dunne of 34a Tiffany Downs, Rochestown Road, Cork, wants to book a Villa in the Canaries with 2 Bedrooms En-Suite including 4 Beds. He would like to have a Swimming Pool on Site, be near the Beach, have at his disposal a TV, Telephone, Garden. He would like to avail of both Room and Cleaning Services. He will not need a Baby-sitter.

TASK 7P

- The following document may be created using a combination of left and right-aligned tabs, or alternatively by using tables.
- Count the rows and columns and create a table with the required number of rows and columns.
- Use double-line spacing.
- Save as 'Dawson MW'.

DAWSON GUILLOTINE

SALES NUMBERS – 1 January to 31 December *Bold*

High-Quality table-top guillotines

MODEL	PRODUCT CODE	1994	1993	1992
Dahle Heavy Duty	SA 23569	23,456	12,345	234,780
Myers Surecut	TP 2344	5,432	44,567	67,890
Hobby Cutter	PY 23429	78,345	45,897	23,432
Commander Lightweight	KL 12765	12,345	78,432	12,556

TASK 13H

- Create the booking form as the primary document.
- Enter variable symbols carefully.
- Proofread carefully and save under the filename WPMG070.
- Enter variables into the data document.
- Proofread and save under the filename WPMG071.
- Merge.
- Save under the filename WPMG072 and print one copy.

To: Tara Leisure Ltd 123 Great William St Dublin 4.

From: Name
        Address

Preferred Date(s) of Holiday

        Enter requirements from the lists below:

Chalet/Bungalow/ Villa / Mobile Home

No of Beds   TV
Bedrooms En-Suite   Telephone
Swimming Pool on Site   Garden

Locality

Majorca/Benidorm/Rimini/ Canaries :

Baby-sitter Required   Room Service
Cleaning Service   Near Beach

Continued Overleaf

TASK 7Q

- Create the following document using the table facility of your WP software.
- Reposition the third column, as illustrated.
- Use double-line spacing.
- Save as 'Briefcases MW'.

Sales of briefcases during the 90's

Sturdy Stitched Handles

Type	Item No.	1992	1993	1994
Flapover Case	R180	12,345	24,567	22,330
RLS Briefcase	EUR 10	56,700	23,456	34,532
Pigskin	S210L	34,560	21,340	12,345
Custom Classic	X10C	45,690	12,345	34,560
Leather Executive	R182 9	890 56,700	32,450	12,345
Custom Split Leather	XP14C	23,450	12,560	23,465

TASK 13G

- Compose the letter that Jane Scott sent to these three officials on 2 April, 1994, taking care to insert the symbols for the variables.

- Enter the variable information in a data file and save appropriately.

- Merge both documents together.

- Proofread carefully.

- Print one copy and create envelopes.

Jane Scott, Proprietor of Hilltop Hotel, Ardmore, Co Waterford, has written to three clients thanking them for their letters of a particular date and acknowledging the reservations they have made for their respective clubs. Miss Scott notes that the person who has made the booking in each case have official positions within that club and have responsibility for holiday bookings. Each group are booking a number of single rooms as well as double rooms en suite. Within each group, some people have opted for full board while others would prefer to have Bed and Breakfast only.

Ms Scott acknowledges booking deposits made. She concludes her letter by saying that she is looking forward to meeting them on their respective dates.

BOOKING 1

Mr Tom Black, O'Growney Terrace, Ballyphehane, Cork, wrote to Hilltop Hotel on the 12 March 1994. He is Secretary of the Ballyphehane Gun Club and their holiday is commencing on Monday, 16 October, 1994. This group wants to book 10 Single rooms and 6 double rooms en suite. 18 want Bed and Breakfast only while remaining 4 want full board. Tom sent on a deposit of £80 when he was making the initial booking.

BOOKING 2

Mr John Smith, of Middle Road, Crosshaven, Co Cork, who is Treasurer of Crosshaven Harriers paid a deposit of £200 on 2 March, 1994, when he made a reservation for Monday, 23 July, 1994. This booking entailed accommodating 40 people in Single Rooms and 12 in Double rooms en suite. 32 of the group have opted for full board but 20 want Bed and Breakfast only.

BOOKING 3

The President of Youghal Golf Club reserved 60 single rooms and 14 double rooms en suite for a holiday commencing Monday, 15 December, 1994. He paid £250 deposit when he made this booking on 16 February, 1994. This reservation includes Full Board for 40 people while the remaining golfers are happy to have Bed and Breakfast only.

- Create the following document using the table facility of your WP software.

- Enhance using the underline and emboldening facilities, as illustrated.

- Use double-line spacing.

- Save as 'Travels MW'.

Travels Abroad / BoLD

<u>Countries Visited</u>: France & Germany

<u>Date</u>	<u>Staff Member</u>	<u>Position</u>	<u>Travel Cost</u>	<u>Travellers Cheques</u>
1 March [OCT] 1994	Marcella Ryan	Supervisor	£2,900	£1,590
4 May 1994	Rita Collins [HOARE]	Trainee Manager	£750	£400
6 June 1994	Michael Foley	Shop Steward	£2,300	£1,250
24 July 1994	John [MICK] Deignan	General Operator	£1,200	£650
28 July [28 OCT MAY] 1994	Peter Mooney	Switchboard Supervisor	£1,500	£1,250

TASK 13F

- Use the Mail Merge procedures of your word processor to create a standard letter and data file, which will incorporate the many variables listed for the four carpet retailers below.

- Proofread carefully and save under appropriate filenames.

- Merge main document and data file together and print one copy of each merged letter.

- Create either labels or envelopes for each letter.

Mr John Grey of 23 Windy Willows, Ennis, Co. Clare, wrote to four Carpet Fitters as follows:

LETTER 1:   He wrote to Mr Tom Doody, Miller's ~~Walk~~ Row, Navan, Co Meath, and thanked him for his quotation number 90876, which was dated 14 May, 1994, for the sum of: £870. Mr Grey said that unfortunately he gave the incorrect measurements for the room in question and explained that they should have been: 12 ft wide by 14 ft long.

LETTER 2:   Mr Grey also wrote to Mr Michael Roberts, of Dunedin, Tramore, Co Waterford. The quotation number here was 87656, dated 23 ~~June~~ MAY 1994, for the sum of £750. The measurements for the room in question should have been: 12.5 ft wide by 13 ft long.

LETTER 3:   Mr John Moore of Miller's Walk, Millstreet, Co Cork was sent a letter also. Mr Moore's original quotation for £450 was numbered: 78654 and was dated: 12 May 1994. The width of the room in question should have read: 11 ft wide by 14 ft long.

LETTER 4:   Mr Grey wrote to: Mr ~~Michael~~ John Foster of Sunrise, Mardyke, Cork, regarding his £650 quotation numbered: 7643 of the 14 ~~January~~ May 1994. The quotation should have been for a room measuring 12 ft wide by 13.5 long.

Mr Grey concludes all letters by apologising for unnecessary bother in the matter and asked for another quotation as soon as possible.

Date the letter: 1 June 1994

TASK 7S

- Create the following menu; choose appropriate fonts.
- Leader dots are combined with the right-aligned tab.
- Save as 'Metropole'.
- Print one copy.

METROPOLE HOTEL AT CHRISTCHURCH
M E N U
DINNER £25 (inc VAT)
Sunday 24 September 2000

Garlic Mushrooms .... *Cream of Chicken Soup*
Crab Claws .... *Warm Duck Salad*
Haddock Mornay

Roast Barbary Duckling
Rack of Connemara Lamb
Loin of Pork Steak
Supreme of Chicken St Elgar

Creamy Cauliflower...*Boiled Potatoes*
Steamed Carrots ....*Roast Potatoes*

Fresh Fruit Salad .... *Baked Alaska*
Lemon Meringue Pie...*Apple Tart*

Cheese and Biscuits
After-Dinner Mints

Tea or Coffee

AMENDMENTS TO MERGED LETTERS

Fuller's Letter

Amend first paragraph to read: 'designing and fitting a wardrobe'. Add another sentence to end of third paragraph: 'We appreciate very much the fact that you passed on our name to your colleagues.'

Lane's Letter

Add a fourth paragraph: 'In view of the fact that you are the widow of our esteemed former partner, you will be eligible for generous discounts.'

O'Brien's Letter

Add a final paragraph: 'Congratulations, you are one of the ten lucky winners in our weekly competition. You will be billed for half of your order only.'

TASK 7T

- Create the following menu; use the right-aligned tabs with leader dots — enhance with appropriate Clip Art.

- Save as 'Burncourt'.

- Print one copy.

Hosfords' of Burncourt

❆❆❆❆❆❆❆❆❆❆❆❆❆

Established 1945
Menu for Monday 11 September 2000

Salad of Home Cured Gravalax **£8.95**
Comamona Smoked Salmon Platter **£9.95**
Garnished with lemon, capers and sliced onion
Comamona Smoked Salmon **£10.95**
Served with white crabmeat or fresh prawns
Prawn Salad **£11.95**
*Fresh prawns cooked in a court bouillon,
served cold with crisp salad leaves, marie rose*

Hot Seafood Selection
Diuilicinni **£8.50**
Steamed Maree mussels with garlic, parsley, onion, cream and wine
Salmon en Filo **£11.95**
Fillet of salmon, sauteed leeks dressed in filo pastry with a fresh chive hollandaise
Seafood Basket **£10.95**
Lightly poached salmon, cod and haddock in a white wine cream with a puppodum basket, duo of sauces
Crab Claws* **£12.50**
Fresh Roundstone crab claws dipped in a fennel batter, served hot with Pernod and garlic butter
Baked Cod .... **£.9.95**
Fillet of cod, with a pimento and mix nut crust, mushroom and smoked bacon sauce
Grilled Supreme of Salmon **£10.95**
Served with a ratatouille of Mediterranean vegetables, lemon and parsley butter
Scallops Mornay **£14.50**
Atlantic scallops lightly cooked in a cheese sauce served with gratinated potatoes
Halibut Steak **£12.50**
Served with fresh pesto, pinenut topping and chive beurre blanc

---

VARIABLES

[1] 900P
[2] 1 June, 1994
[3] Mrs Monica Fuller, 34 Baker's Hill, Kinsale, Co Cork
[4] Mrs Fuller
[5] 28 May
[6] John Walsh
[7] Wednesday, 14 June, 1994
[8] 11.00 a.m.

[1] 9876H
[2] 15 March, 1994
[3] Ms Breda Lane, 24 Miller's Bush, Cobh, Co Cork
[4] Ms Lane
[5] 12 March 1994
[6] Larry Quirke
[7] 22 March, 1994
[8] 12.00 noon

[1] K8976
[2] 20 May 1994
[3] Mr John Lamb, 12 Lover's Walk, Tivoli, Cork
[4] Mr Lamb
[5] 14 May,1994
[6] Kerry Moore
[7] 20 May, 1994
[8] 11.00 a.m.

[1] 7689OP
[2] 16 June, 1994
[3] Mr Bob Walker, 65 O'Donnell Row, Youghal, Co Cork
[4] Mr Walker
[5] 12 June 1994
[6] Frank Jordan
[7] 20 July,1994
[8] 10.00 a.m.

Unit 8

Headers and Footers

Page Numbering

Hyphenation

Headings

Bullets

Numbering

TASK 13E

- Create the standard letter below; use margins of 1.25".
- Use Spell Check, proofread carefully and save under the filename 'Letters 76'.
- Key in variables into a separate file; save as 'Names 2001'.
- Merge letters to screen and make amendments to Fuller's and Lane's letters as indicated below.
- Print the letters on A4 paper.
- Print four labels.

Ref [1]

Date [2]

[3]

Dear [4]

Thank you for your letter dated [5] about an estimate for designing and fitting a bedroom.

If convenient to you, [6], our Chief Estimator, will visit you on [7] at [8] to consider your suggestion and offer his advice.

Please let us know if the suggested date and time are convenient to you.

Yours sincerely

A MILLER
Department Manager

Guidelines

1. Headers and Footers

This feature is used for adding text that repeats at the top of each page (header) or at the bottom of each page (footer).
The WP software may also offer the option of displaying the header/footer on every page/odd page/even page. Header/footer features may also allow the addition of current time, current date or page number.

2. Page Numbering

This feature allows the insertion and alignment of page numbers within a header/footer. You may choose to either show or hide the page number on the first page.

3. Hyphenation

Hyphenation reduces the ragged appearance of unjustified text and allows you to fit more text on to a page. In justified text, hyphenation reduces the amount of space inserted between words to fill out a line.

4. Headings

There are two other styles of paragraph headings — shoulder and paragraph. (Main Headings were studied in Unit 5.)

Shoulder Headings: These are usually typed in CLOSED capitals at the left-hand margin; they are preceded and followed by one line space. There is no punctuation used when typing main or shoulder headings, unless the last word is abbreviated. The underscore may be used with both types of headings.
Paragraph Headings: These may be typed in CLOSED capitals with or without the underscore, or they may be typed in lower case with initial capitals and using the underscore. Paragraph headings may run into the first sentence of the paragraph, with or without punctuation.

5. Bullets

You can quickly add bullets to existing lines of text, or you can automatically create bulleted lists as you type.
Select the bullets feature — a standard bullet appears at the left margin, type the text. Alternatively, highlight or type text and then select the bullet feature — a bullet is applied to the current paragraph or paragraphs.
Clicking on the bullet symbol again will turn off the bullet feature. WP software offers a variety of bullets, including arrows, stars etc.

6. Numbering

You can quickly add numbers to existing lines of text, or you can automatically create numbered lists as you type. The procedure is the same as for bullets.
The numbering feature can be removed from the text by clicking on the numbering symbol again. WP software includes a variety of numbering, e.g. large Roman numerals I, II, III, IV; small Roman numerals i, ii, iii, iv.

[1] AT/GH
[2] 21 February, 1994
[3] John Wilson, 4 King's Row, Manorhamilton, Co Down
[4] Mr Wilson
[5] K897665
[6] Drawer Cabinets
[7] 6 March, 1994

[1] AT/KL
[2] 25 May, 1994
[3] Barry O'Brien, 34 Dyke Parade, Cork
[4] Mr O'Brien
[5] L78654
[6] 10 Energy-saving Desk Lights
[7] 12 June, 1994

[1] AT/MP
[2] 2 June, 1994
[3] John Roche, Fair St, Mallow, Co Cork
[4] Mr Roche
[5] P9854
[6] 20 Custom-built Dressers
[7] 23 June, 1994

AMENDMENTS TO MERGED LETTERS

Foster's Letter

Add another sentence to the end of first paragraph: 'We were delighted to hear that you were thrilled with the quality of the previous delivery.'

Wilson's Letter

Replace last paragraph with: 'In view of your unsatisfactory track record with our company, we regret that we were unable to fulfil your order last week, but we are now happy to despatch order on [7].'

O'Brien's Letter

Add a final paragraph: 'Congratulations, you are one of the ten lucky winners in our weekly competition. You will be billed for half of your order only.'

TASK 8A

- Create the following document, which is an example of a paragraph heading.
- Use single-line spacing on A5 landscape paper.
- Set margins as follows: left at 1.5", right at 1".
- Font type is to be Arial Black, font size 12.
- Save as 'Meteor MW'.

COURT RULES IN METEOR FAVOUR

Awarding of third mobile licence

SUPREME COURT The decision yesterday taken in the Supreme Court clears the way for the award of the State's third mobile phone licence to Meteor Communications. The five-judge court unanimously upheld an appeal by the Office of the Director of Telecommunications.

MONETARY TERMS Meteor has claimed the legal proceedings have cost it millions of pounds. Although the regulators announced in October 1998 the decision to award Meteor the licence, it has been delayed pending the outcome of the action.

TASK 13D

- Create the letters below (1" margins) — they have many variables.
- Save under the filename 'Order 55'.
- Make amendments suggested in the merged documents.
- Print letters on A4 paper.
- Create envelopes.

Our ref: [1]

[2]

[3]

Dear [4]

We acknowledge receipt of your order number [5] for [6].
This order will be despatched on [7].

Yours faithfully

ADDRESSEES AND OTHER VARIABLES

Data Source 1

[1] AT/WT
[2] 20 January, 1994
[3] Milly Foster, Main St, Cloyne, Co Cork
[4] Ms Foster
[5] J7895
[6] Folding Tables
[7] 5 February, 1994

TASK 8B

- Create the following document, which is another example of a paragraph heading.
- Use single-line spacing on A5 landscape paper.
- Set both margins to 2.54 cm.
- Font type is to be changed to Times New Roman, font size 10.
- Save as 'Innovation MW'.
- Print one copy.

NATIONAL INNOVATION AWARDS

GREAT BUSINESS IDEAS REWARDED

Selc Ireland, the winners of the small business category last year continues to expand. It now employs 52 people, putting it firmly in the medium-sized category. Selc forecast that turnover will increase by more than £1 million in the current year, while the last year has seen a growth of some £750,000 in turnover.

Lisbaun Industrial Park in Galway now houses a sophisticated lab. While this development is in line with what the parent company set out to do, time-lighting control products have been one of the mainstays of Selc's business over the years.

TASK 13C continued

- Set up the data source — it has 8 sets of variables.
- Save as 'Members 2000'.
- Merge with the previous letter and print labels.

The following members are to be circularised:

Ms Joan Burton
Sea View Lawn
Ardmore
Co Waterford

Ms Hilda Beatty
12 Lifford Close
Ardmore
Co Waterford

Mr Jim Gleeson
'St Jude's'
56 Upper John St
Ardmore
Co Waterford

Mr William Bond
35 Carr's Hill
Ardmore
Co Waterford

Mr Killian Deasy
23 Hill View
Ardmore
Co Waterford

Ms Lena Long
Ardmore
Co Waterford

Ms Delia Grace
'St Anthony's'
Daunt Square
Ardmore
Co Waterford

Mr John Finnegan
'St Martin's'
45 The Wharf
(Northside)
Ardmore
Co Waterford

TASK 8C

- Create the following exercise using shoulder headings.

- Use single-line spacing on A4 landscape paper.

- Set both margins to 2.5 cm.

- Font type is to be changed to Arial Black, font size 12.

- Save as 'Stock Market MW'.

- Print one copy on A4 landscape paper.

ANALYSING THE STOCK MARKET

The Psychology of the Stock Market

BATTLE OF WATERLOO

Rothschild made a fortune from the battle of Waterloo. He knew the allies had won while the London stock market was awash with rumours of defeat and flight. He bought government stock at rock bottom prices and made a killing when it was realized that Napoleon had been defeated.

LONG TERM CREDIT FUND

David Coher does not subscribe to the view of John Meriweather and his Long Term Credit fund, which developed a series of complex calculations to predict market prices and was a phenomenal success from 1987 to 1998. However, when the fall came, the company went wallop, almost causing a world recession and Alan Greenspan, who organized the rescue of Long Term Credit, to describe it as the "most terrifying period in international finance".

TASK 13C

- Key in the following draft letter.
- Save as 'Tennis'.

---

*
*
*
*
*

Dear *

Munster Tennis Players' Tournament

As the newly elected ~~captain~~ President of Waterpoint Lawn Tennis Club, I want to cordially invite you to register for the above competition. As you know, this tournament is held annually to prepare players for the summer circuit. Successful players in the past have gone on to win many significant matches both nationally and locally

Looking forward to meeting you later in the season.

Yours sincerely

John Forde

~~HONORARY CAPTAIN~~
PRESIDENT

TASK 8D

- Create the following exercise using shoulder headings.

- Use double-line spacing on A4 portrait paper.

- Set both margins to 1.5".

- Font type is to be changed to Arial, font size 10.

- Save as 'Stamp MW'.

- Print one copy.

INTERNATIONAL ELECTRONIC STAMP

IRISH TEAM FIRST TO POST

Black Stamp

As this month marks the 160th anniversary of the first use of the Penny Black stamp for postage, it is appropriate an Irish development team is conducting a first postal issue of its own, electronically. Irish postal applications company, Anshe, which was recently purchased by Escher, a US founded postal technology company for an estimated £15 million, is behind the commercial development of an electronic franking system for the Singapore post office network.

Document authentication

Not only does the electronic franking system offer an alternative to the traditionally costly franking machine for small and medium-sized enterprises, it also features an ingenious means of document authentication. Each envelope also carries a small digital barcode, or electronic indicia, featuring unique component details of a snapshot of a section of that envelope's make-up.

TASK 13B continued

- Set up the data source — it has four sets of variables.
- Save as 'Names 56'.
- Merge with the previous letter.
- Print out envelopes.

VARIABLES

LETTER 1

[1] Ms Kitty Donovan

O'Donovan's Road
CORK

 [2] Kitty

LETTER 2

[1] Ms Sheila Cunningham
Friar's Walk
Ballyphehane
CORK

[2] Sheila

LETTER 3

[1] Mr Matt Dorgan
Knocklyon Road
Rathfarnham
DUBLIN 16

[2] Matt

LETTER 4

[1] Mr John Walsh
'St Jude's'
Victoria Avenue
MILLSTREET
Co Cork

[2] John

TASK 8E

- Create the following document; follow the instructions for layout.
- Use font Times New Roman, font size 12 and 1" margins.
- Set up the header and footer suggested.
- Save as 'Advertisement MW'.
- Print one copy.

ADVERTISEMENT — BOLD & SPACED CAPS.
ACCESS ACCOUNTS — ITALICS

Fully-featured accounts software for Windows

General comments: Access accounts for Windows is a modular multi-featured accounts package that is definitely NOT for the faint hearted. Developed by UK-based Access Accounting, the software was until recently marketed as Pegasus for Windows. PACKAGE

↑ Bold ↓

Unique Design: It was designed for large scale operations rather than small businesses. Access has nine main modules including Sales Ledger, Nominal Ledger, Purchase Ledger, Cash Book, Credit Control etc.

[Dbl Spacing]

There are also a number of additional modules and utilities including Ad-Hoc Report Generator, Forms Designer and Import Utility

Create the Header: " Access can handle up to 10 prices for each stock item", and the Footer: " Access has all the attributes of windows software"
CENTRE BOTH

TASK 13B

- Key in the following draft letter.
- Save as 'Hostel'.

13 June 1994

[1]

Dear [2]

Thank you for your recent letter. of THE 10.

I was very sorry to hear that you were unsuccessful in your bid for O'Reilly's Hostel. I suppose it was inevitable that the Williams family would be interested in this property given their considerable investment in the south-side of the city.

Do contact me the next time you are in town.

Every good wish

Joan Whelan

TASK 8F

- Set up the following document with 1" margins.
- Set up the header as shown.
- Save as 'Reuters Agency MW'.
- Set up a footer with a page number, as displayed below.
- Fully justify and apply the hyphenation feature.
- Save under a new name 'Strategic Rocket Unit MW'.
- Print one copy on A4 paper.

Reuters Agency Report

Pranksters net a year in prison

Two Russians were sentenced to a year each in prison for posing on the Internet as renegade nuclear rocket commanders with plans to wipe out cities in Europe.

The two had posted messages claiming to be officers at a strategic rocket unit, driven to the edge by the harsh realities of post-Soviet life, who would launch a nuclear strike on European cities if their demands were not met, a news agency reported.

The hoax triggered the alarm of the US FBI and police in Austria which both asked Russia to investigate. The two were convicted under statute that outlaws alarmist hoaxes causing material damage or danger to the public.

Internet Pranksters	*1*

TASK 13A

- Key in the letter below; save as 'Merge letter'.
- Set up the data source which comprises of two addresses; save as 'Names 99'.
- Merge the letter with the document containing variables.

---

11 May 1994

[1]

Dear [2]

I refer to your recent telephone call to this office regarding the ~~three~~ _four_-bedroom house recently advertised by us.

I regret to inform you that this Sale has now been cancelled. The owner has withdrawn his property from the market.

Yours sincerely

VARIABLES

LETTER 1

[1]   Mr John Walters
      Main St
      KILLEAGH
      Co Cork

[2]   Mr Walters

LETTER 2

[1]   Ms Mary Curran
      Fair St
      MALLOW
      Co Cork

[2]   Ms Curran

TASK 8G

- Set up the following document with:

  Line spacing
  Indentation
  Header/Footer
  Page numbering, as suggested.

- Save as 'Initial Font MW'.

CHANGING THE DOCUMENT INITIAL FONT.

(as the default font for the printer)

(Dbl spacing
1.25" margins)

Normally the initial starting font for a document is whatever font is chosen. This feature
is really good when used in conjunction with relative sizes. You must choose a font from a
list of available fonts [If you want to use a different starting font for a document,]

(Single sp.
Indent 2")

Suppose you want to print a document in a ~~small~~ very small print size, but want to see
it on the screen with larger letters, you could start by choosing
a large print size as the document's initial font.

It Use only relative sizing to change print sizes [As you type the document,] Before printing
your document, change the document's initial font to the smaller size.

THE OFFICE

Working Conditions

(a) Ventilation   Many offices are air-conditioned. It is essential that staff
have well ventilated rooms, in which to work.

(b) Heating Offices should be ~~warmed~~ adequately heated so that staff are ~~comfortable~~ warm without
being suffocated.

(c) Lighting Many offices use artificial light.

(Number the page : 37)

(Right align)

(Dbl spacing
1.25" margins)

Header: Complement your Word Processor
with a Deluxe Ink Jet Printer
from Sadlers
Footer: Sadlers for Quality and Service

Unit 8   87

Guidelines

1. Merging Documents

On Screen Merge involves three processes:
The creation of a main document, which contains the text that remains the same from document to document.
The creation of a data source, which contains the information that varies from document to document (variables).
The merging of the main document with the data source.
When the main document (usually known as the primary document) is merged with the data source (may be called the secondary document), personalised forms, letters, labels, envelopes etc, can be created.

Note: Basic variables, such as name and address are used in the On Screen Merge exercises in this Unit.

2. Envelopes

The addressees' names and addresses should be typed in the same font in single-line spacing with blocked layout as in the letters.

Settings should be set so that the details will appear on the envelope — halfway down and a third of the way across.

3. Labels

Use the facility within the WP software to set up labels.
Choose from the defined sheets, which are structured in 8 x 3 or 7 x 3 labels per sheet.

TASK 8H

- Set up the following three-page document with:

  Line spacing
  Indentation
  Header/Footer — making changes on each page will involve, with Word for Windows, for example, creating section breaks and breaking the link between the header and footer from one page to the next.
  Page numbering, as suggested.

- Save as 'Technical Support MW'.

Technical Support Hotline ← Spaced Caps

At the heart of gifco, you'll find our valuable service. [These include our _and support systems_ NP award winning technical support hotline at the end of the phone with immediate access to the history of your system, who will spend as long as it takes to ~~solve the riddle~~ put the problem right.

The service is available free, 8am to 8pm, Monday to Friday, every day of the week with a low cost option to extend to 24 hours, 7 days a week. _seven_

We're in direct telephone contact with 40,000 of our customers per day world-wide, so we're constantly aware of what makes our systems work best. [The result is ready-to-go computing solution designed NP by 40,000 experts. _run on_

By cutting out the middleman and the overheads, you get a lot more for your money with customer satisfaction.

(They are ready to run.) It's all very simple. gifco have created a choice of systems designed to cover all your needs.

At gifco, we put you firmly in control. You can choose the system that suits you best - Our "ready-to-run" range with pre-loaded software packages featuring industry leading business applications.

Then there's our CD media systems, access and sound to the latest CD-Rom technology. A selection of our _most popular_ systems are featured here, each of which represents exceptional value.

Call us for further information on these _and others_ in our complete range and we'll be happy to talk to you.

(Use Hyphenation feature & 12-Pitch)

Header: Your most frequently requested PC Systems
Footer: GIFCO - The Way Forward!!
Page 1

Unit 13

Merging Documents

Envelopes

Labels

(Header2) → The New Way to Communicate

PC Solutions

Not only do we design, ~~develop~~ and manufacture your computing solutions, we also provide the support, (WHENEVER YOU NEED IT) ~~you need~~ to keep them running as smoothly as possible. ~~Maybe that's why~~ We're the fastest growing PC company in the Fortune 500. RUN ON

We're also the 5th largest PC manufacturer in the world with a global revenue in excess of $2 billion a year.

It all adds up to a company that is dedicated to your business by making life easier for you and your staff.

The Mobile

ERM is the new wave in advanced cellular communications. Now there's one mobile telephone for all of Europe, offering you digital speech quality, mobility, privacy, security, and the capacity to communicate across the European network.

Avail of our special offer now. If you're already a cellular user, why not trade-up your current model to a new GSM cellular phone. The special £800 price of ~~£995~~ includes a phone, car-kit with booster, plus installation and connection to the Eircell network.

Footer: Digital Clients Page 2

Dbl spacing
HANGING PAR.

Make that call!

From 1st September there is a change in the way telephone calls are charged. The cost per unit is being reduced from 11.17p to 9.5p and the time interval for each unit is changing.

An example of a typical bill is given here. Your bill, however, will include only the relevant types of calls you made during the billing period. Your calls are separated to show those made up to 31st August and those from 1st September onwards.

This leaflet should help you understand the way the new changes will appear on your bill.

✗ Local Calls
From 1st September, local calls made between 8 a.m. and 6 p.m. on Mondays to Fridays inclusive will be charged in units of 3 minutes. Calls made between 6 p.m. and 8 a.m,. Mondays to Fridays, and all day Saturdays, will be charged in units of 15 minutes.

✗ Local (Pre 1/9/93)
Local calls made before 1st September are grouped together irrespective of the call duration.

✗ Local (1 Unit)
Local calls of 1 unit made from 1st September 1993 are shown separately. the cost per unit is 9.5p.

Local (2 to 4 Units)

Telecom Eireann **Telephone Account**   Service
Account Enquiries Dial 198

Account Number
John Walsh
Main St
Dublin
01 *5234321*

Account Type:
BUSINESS

Main Telephone Number
01 8787873

ISSUE DATE
12/12/95   *Rental* **From** 12/12/95 **to** 11/01/96
Calls **From** 11/11/95 to 9/12/95

ACCOUNT SUMMARY

LAST BILL AMOUNT   290

PAYMENTS RECEIVED
THANK YOU⋅   £290.00 Cr

LINE RENTAL: £30.00
EQUIPMENT RENTAL: £10.00

CALLS		UNITS	RATE
540	LOCAL	725	0.1117
312	LOCAL	312	0.0950
96	LOCAL	205	0.0950
10	INLAND	34	0.1117
6	C. CHNL	105	0.1117
3	INTERN.	36	0.0950

ACCESS If you wish to pay this Account by
VISA   Total: 149.02
                              E.&O.E.
CREDIT CARD DIAL FREEFONE: **1800 222222**

PAYMENT DUE BY 26/12/95

Local ✗
Local calls of more than 4 units are summarised as shown

Inland/Cross Channel/Intern. ✗
The long distance inland, cross channel shown at a unit rate of 11.17p were made up to the end of last month.

Premium Rate ✗
These are the calls to one of the 1550 XXXXX Premium Rate Special Service calls shown at a unit rate of 11.17p were made up to the end of last. month.

Directory Enquiries ✗
Directory Enquiry calls cost 28.5 p each. You are allowed 2 free directory enquiry calls per monthly bill These free calls are identified as Directory Credits40

VAT ✗
The Current Rate of VAT is 21%. All prices in this leaflet are exclusive of VAT.

Times New Roman (5)

Page 2

THE WONDERS OF THE MODERN WORLD ← *Header*

informational or educational software

Multimedia – is it all just hot air?

~~yardstick~~ del

The interactivity Λ of any communications Λis an important ~~measuring stick~~ in rating it as multimedia – in fact, it is every bit as important as the aural and visual information it imparts.

yardstick

Indent 1.5" from both margins – single sp.

The multimedia concept is being hyped beyond all belief. It seems that most of the people making all the waves in this particular pond can't even agree on a ~~interpretation~~ of what multimedia means.

definition

Clearly, multimedia refers to a new, complex kind of media product. Its perspectives are interesting. The applications and methods used are machinery, just like any other / new media

and indeed conventional

TOTALLY CONVINCING

DOUBLE SPACING

With 300 new features in the~~the~~thoroughly overhauled user interface, every tool needed to make ~~enthralling~~ presentations is here.

captivating

There are all kinds of precision aid to help you to design perfect presentations. These include features such as automatic kerning, object orientation features, and new user-definable rulers.

The totally redesigned user interface makes work quick. You get free-floating palettes moved to the position of your choice. This simplifies operations and increases your productivity.

Instead of having to scroll laboriously through pop-up menus,

faster

Multimedia Hype   Page 3

TASK 12H

- Set up the following two-page document — the first page is in landscape format.
- Save as 'Telecom'.
- Create suggested headers and footers and make editing changes.
- Resave and print one copy.

[Handwritten: Bold Script MT (24)]

Explaining your telephone bill layout

A guide for business customers *[Handwritten: Helv (14)]*

TELECOM EIREANN *[Handwritten: Courier (16)]*

[Handwritten: Ireland's Telephone Co. — Bold Script MT (20)]

[Handwritten: Page 1 — Script (24)]

---

*[Handwritten: Insert 'Dear Sir' after all headings *]*

Call Details Availability *[Handwritten: Helv (11)]*
Details of calls will not be available to the same extent for all customers. There are two exceptions which apply:-

Metered Calls
Less than 10% of our telephone lines are connected to telephone exchanges where detailed billing is not available. In these cases the number of calls and units for all direct dialled calls is recorded on a meter in the exchange and billed as metered calls on the account. Meter readings were taken at the end of August and consequently calls made prior to the meter reading date are charged at 11.17p per unit.

Digital Exchanges
Details of all trunk and international calls have been available for some time for all customers connected to digital exchanges. A list of the telephone numbers affected is on the next page.

Further Information
Customers are connected to exchanges with detailed billing facilities.

[Handwritten: Make that call!] *[Handwritten: Helv (10)]*

TELEPHONE NUMBERS AFFECTED	From	COMPLETION DATE FOR LOCAL CALLS
DUBLIN 01	340500	340599	25 Nov '93
CORK 021	281100	281199	17 Dec '93
	284200	284215	
	285200	285209	
	30000	328229	
	329000	329999	24 Sept '93
	391000	399999	17 Dec '93
GALWAY 091	39000	391999	15 Oct '93
	86000	86099	
	750000	769999	
	770000	770999	
DUBLIN 01	50000		23 Nov '93
	52000		
	59000		

TASK 8I

- Set up the following two-page document with:

    Line spacing
    Indentation
    Header/Footer
    Page numbering, as suggested.

- Save as 'Builders MW'.

COMPLO BUILDERS PROVIDERS

LOCATION: Complo Builders Providers Ltd at Hare's View, Triskel Avenue, Cork, has rapidly established itself as a company with a leading edge when it comes to service and price.

HOME DECORATOR: The home decorator is catered for with a large selection of both (interior) and (exterior) paints. The colour choice system available offers more than 2,000 shades. There is as well a comprehensive hardware section with an excellent choice of hand tools to suit all needs.

PRODUCTS: Product availability, delivery and back up is an area in which this expanding company is extremely strong. There is an extensive and impressive product range, and the company caters for the Do It Yourself enthusiast and the home decorator. at the Complo Builders u.c. Providers, you will find ample parking. The range of products available at Complo Builders Providers is huge. Drainage products including both (PVC) and (cast iron) alkathnies, rough timber, flue liners, oil tanks from Rom Plastics and so on are in the yards. (for sale)

BATHROOMS: There is a lovely display of bathroom suites. A working whirlpool bath is a feature of this area and there are working models of various types of shower valves. Rita Moore is available to help customers with their bathroom designs and colour schemes.

PRICE QUALITY AND SERVICE

TUBES: Copper   Quality Copper tube comes with a 30-year guarantee. All of the copper tube carries a unique 25 year guarantee and is manufactured to IS238 : 1980.

BOILERS: Firebird   Manufacturers of Oil and Solid Fuel appliances including Popular 90 and Super Q Kitchen Model Oil Boiler. Supreme Backboilers are available from all local merchants

Italics

(on both pages)   Header: Complo for Quality
                   Footer: Complo - Specialists in: Building
                           Materials | Plumbing | Bathroom Suites
                           & fittings

TASK 12G

- Set up the following three-column document.
- Save as 'Apple Information'.
- Create suggested headers and footers and make editing changes.
- Resave and print one copy.

[handwritten: Arial rounded MT (14)]

Call the Apple information Centre now! — *[handwritten: Header]*

[handwritten: Helv (26) Bold]

Power Macintosh

For all of its futuristic qualities, Power Macintosh comes with a price that's firmly rooted in the economics of today.

That is, you can own a power *[handwritten: uc]* Macintosh for as little as £1,345 ex. VAT). It comes with built-in Ethernet networking, file-sharing software sound and up to 24-bit colour display support.

Add Apple AV technologies and you can record video to *[handwritten: Helv (14)]* your hard disk drive, simply by plugging a standard camcorder.

Or export presentations from your Power Macintosh to video tape for easy distribution.

Or use your Power Macintosh as a communications centre to send faxes or to send and receive data. You can even conduct desk-to desk video conferences over a local area network.

In the future, you'll be able to use Plain Talk, our voice recognition technology, to tell you computer what to do.

[handwritten: Helv (12) Italic Bold]

Nobody expected a computer to make you this productive.

Among all personal computers, Macintosh remains unique in its ability to get the job done.

A recent study by Arthur D. Little confirms what Apple has been saying for years; people who use Macintosh computers tend to do more and do it faster than people who use PCs.

In the study, Macintosh users completed a set of business computing task in 44% less time than a comparable set of PC users running Windows to do the same task.

The overall result is a computer system that, year in and year out, has proven significantly less expensive to support and maintain.

Nobody expected it to be so easy to upgrade to Power Macintosh

Millions of Macintosh users can upgrade to Power Macintosh for as little as £785 (ex VAT) Of course, a Power Macintosh can work with any Macintosh computers you already own –sharing files and information easily over a network.

[handwritten: Times New Roman (9)]

Power Mac.	6100/60	7100/66	
Proc.	Power PC 601	Power PC 601	Power PC 601
Speed	60 MHz	66 MHz	80 MHz
Mem.	8 MB Exp. to 72 MB	8 MB Exp. to 246 MB	8 MB Exp. to 136 MB
Expan Slots	1 PDS or NuBus	3 NuBus	3 NuBus
HD Storage	160 MB or 250 MB	250 MB or 500 MB	500 MB or 1GB
Dis. Supp.	DRAM	DRAM	DRAM
Netwk	Ethernet	Local Talk	Ethernet
Retail Prices from (Ex VAT)	£1540	£1740	£1840

All this plus built-in Macintosh PC Exchange AppleScript Quick Time True/Type fonts, GeoPort serial ports, 16-bit stereo audio input. output, file-sharing without a dedicated server and more.

[handwritten: Arial (12) Bold]

CONVERSIONS : Lofts   Imagine a bedroom upstairs in your roof space or any other kind of room for that matter. If you have an attic why not put it to good use?

With a high quality loft conversion using VELUX roof windows, you can creat beautiful new rooms, expanding your living space and the value of your property.

So why not find out more? ✓ For lots of good ideas and a free estimate, simply dial your local VELUX window installer on the number below;

PHONE NOW FOR YOUR FREE ESTIMATE
G WALSH & SONS
25 FIRS PLACE
EDINBURGH EH6 7EZ
Tel: 031 565 8975

BOILERS :   Glow worm   Simple, efficient with cast iron reliability, the new Ultimate cast-iron hung boilers
                              are ideal for new or replacement heating systems, because they are compatible with
              Italics   all types of systems — gravity fed, fully pumped ore even sealed systems with
                              balanced flue models.

With heat outputs rated from 20,000 to 80,000 Btu/h, plus the installation flexibility, the Ultimate range will suit all types of property and system (new or old).

Congratulations to
Bold   COMPLO BUILDERS PROVIDERS   ⋏ #
              Harrington   ⋏ #
        Ireland's No.1 Supplier
        of garage Doors

        Also Available
        Industrial and
        Domestic Sliding gear and
        Hanley Hardware — A Complete Range

        P C Harrington (Irl) Ltd
        Westlink Industrial Estate   Italics
        Kylemore Road
          Dublin 10
        Tel. 01 645989

BORD FAILTE PROMOTION — *amiol (rr)*

boodma old style (rr4)

ROYAL GUNPOWDER MILLS
Ballincollig

Visitors will experience a taste of what life was like working in a gunpowder factory during the 19th century. The visitors' centre incorporates a main display area with educational panels, models and an interesting audio-visual. the guided tour through the canal and tree-lined complex leads to a full working 'Incorporating Mill' powered by a water wheel.

CHARLES FORT
Kinsale

Constructed in the early 1680s in honour of King Charles II by William Robinson, architect of the Royal Hospital in Kilmainham, Dublin. Charles Fort situated on the eastern side of Kinsale is a classic example of star-shaped fort. In use until 1921, it gives a unique insight into Irish fortifications. situated near to the charming village of Summer Cove, Charles Fort offers the ideal holiday location.

WEST CORK MODEL VILLAGE
Clonakilty

The West Cork Model Village offers a miniature representation of West Cork towns during the 30s to 50s period. Numerous animated scenes and a fully automated model of the West Cork Railway are sure to captivate you. The atmosphere is further enhanced by the 40s railway building.

FRENCH ARMADA
Bantry

In the winter of 1796 a formidable French Armada inspired by Theobald Wolfe Tone sailed from Brest in France to invade Ireland. Almost 50 warships carried nearly 15,000 soldiers to the south-west coast of Ireland. housed in a restored stable block adjacent to Bantry House, the centre, through the use of exciting illustrations and set piece displays, recounts the epic story of the ill-fated French expedition as it occurred on those fateful days and nights.

CORK AIRPORT' *amiol hostel MT (rd)*

Aer Rianta

The new vastly improved passenger terminal at Cork Airport is considered by man to be the jewel in the crown of the Irish airports. Marble fountains and aquaria containing tropical fish are placed around the building to relax and entertain its customers, while an open coal fire in the arrivals hall conveys a real sense of Irish welcome.

script (ro)

2

THE QE LINER DOCKS IN COBH ON AUGUST 5

Unit 9

Reports

Financial Statements

Flow Charts

Organisational Charts

TASK 12F

- Set up the following two-page, three-column document on landscape paper.
- Save as 'Aer Rianta'.
- Set up headers and footers and apply suggested font types and sizes.
- Resave and print one copy.

JAMESON HERITAGE CENTRE
Serif (12) Midleton

The award winning Jameson Heritage Centre is a lovingly restored 18th century distillery. Visitors are shown an audio-visual presentation, and a guided tour through the old distillery. The tour culminates in the Jameson Bar, where all visitors invited to sample the world-famous Jameson Whiskey (minerals for children) Afterwards, you can visit the gift or coffee shop.

THE QUEENSTOWN STORY
Cobh

Cobh's unique origins, history and legacy is now shown in a multi-media permanent exhibition in the restored Victorian Railway Station and Customs Hall. This award-winning centre traces the story of Irish emigration via Cobh on sailing ships, early steamers and great ocean liners. Relive the dramas of the ill-fated Titanic and Lusitania. Afterwards you can visit the restaurant or browse through the gift shop.

CORK HERITAGE PARK
Cork City

Cork Heritage Park is situated bedside a picturesque estuary of Cork harbour. Located in a restored courtyard, amidst the beautiful landscaped ground of the old Pike estate at Bessboro, Blackrock. Visitors are given an exciting and varied introduction to the rich heritage of Cork. This historic journey covers the Pike contributions, Quaker influence, ecology of the area, the fire service and Cork's maritime traditions.

CORK CITY GAOL
Cork City

Despite its majestic appearance, this prison building housed 19th century prisoners, often in wretched conditions. Furnished cells, amazingly lifelike characters, sound effects and fascinating exhibitions allow the visitor to experience day to day life for prisoners and gaoler. Incorporated in the Gaol visit is a spectacular sound and image presentation.

BLARNEY CASTLE
Blarney

This historic castle is situated near Cork and is world famous for the Blarney stone, which has the traditional power of conferring eloquence on all who kiss it. The word Blarney was introduced into the English language by Queen Elizabeth. She used it to describe entertaining conversation that was possibly not all true. To kiss the stone, set beneath the battlements wall, one has to lean backwards from the parapet walk.

BLARNEY HOUSE
Blarney

Blarney House is a fine example of a baronial house with distinguished architectural features. The interior has been painstakingly restored and features a grand stairwell. It is situated in exquisite gardens incorporating a beautiful view of Blarney Lake. Between the House and the Castle is the stableyard with a display of veteran farm machinery.

THE QE LINER DOCKS IN COBH ON AUGUST 5

Guidelines

1. Reports

Generally, use single-line spacing with double-line spacing between paragraphs.
Set the left margin at 1", except when allowing for binding on the left, then set at
1.5". Set the right margin at a minimum .5".
Top and bottom margins should be set at 1" and the right not less than 1".
However, if the report is to be bound on the left side leave 1.5".
Number all pages except the first page — pages may be numbered at the top or
bottom, at the left or right margin, or centred.
Layout must be constant. If using headings and sub-headings they must be
consistently used with consistent spacing.

2. Financial Statements

The style used for any financial statement will be dictated by the type of material in
the statement and the number and width of the columns.
Generally, the layout of the copy will be the layout used.
Headings and totals must be keyed on the same horizontal line in a two-sided
column layout. A line may be included in the middle of the statement to
distinguish one side from the other; alternatively leave extra spaces to indicate a
division. All figures must be checked for accuracy.

3. Flow Charts

Flow charts are used to illustrate the succession of steps in a procedure.

4. Organisational Charts

Organisational charts indicate hierarchical structure within a company's personnel.

TASK 12E

- Key in the following text.
- Save as 'PC is Tops'.
- Edit as suggested.
- Apply a three-column layout.
- Set up headers and footers.
- Apply suggested fonts.
- Resave.

386 PC Is Tops — *Helv (20)*

Helv (12)

The results of the fourth annual CompuVox survey of the Irish PC market underlines the considerable surge in sales of 386 and 386SX-based PCs in 1993. In all, sales of PCs based on these platforms accounted for two-thirds of the total PC shipments last year.

In contrast, 286-based systems - which predominated in the previous year's survey - accounted for just 3% (386SX PCs for 20%) evidence of the rapid pace at which advancing technology renders earlier designs obsolete.

The survey measures annual sales through the principal Irish distributor channels, and is the only comprehensive local audit of the overall market, covering a variety of topics including PCs, printers, modems, CD ROMS and network operating systems. Whilst individual market shares and detailed results are confidential to each participant, copies of the generic survey report, which indicate trends and market size, can be purchased from CompuVox's sales department on 01 834 56566

I B M (36) — Script

At a world-wide announcement in Switzerland last month, IBM's PC Co reinforced its notebook and server lines with more than a dozen Intel 486's. microprocessor-based computers, most of which are available world-wide immediately. These include a pair of ThinkPad notebooks, a new series in IBM's ValuePoint line, a PS/2 server and two PS/2s.

Courier — (12)

IBM boosts range with new PCs

Helv (18)

Together the new offerings - which include advanced technology such as Intel's fastest 486 processors and Peripheral Component Interconnect (PCI) bus architectures - span both commercial and corporate markets.

The new ThinkPad models are built around the success of IBM's 750. They include many of the same features as the 750. The new models feature more screen options, greater storage capacity and faster 486 processors.

CompuVox — Brush Script MT (20)

TASK 9A

- Create the following report.
- Save as 'Wines 2001'.

CELLAR WINE

Semillon

1.   WHITE WINE

1.1   General description

A white wine with body and flavour - a half-way house for the lighter meats that will bridge the gap between summery salads and full-blooded winter beef.

It's an oddball, really - one of the great, unsung heroes of the wine world which has only itself to blame for its shadowy profile. It's hard to find and even harder to understand. It's far more common to see Semillon credited on labels alongside some other grape than standing alone.

1.2   Blends

Pleasant as blends like Semillon-Chardonnay and Semillon-Sauvignon may be, these duets aren't half as intriguing as a solo performance.

a)   Semillon is a stand-alone wine.
b)   It is a New World phenomenon.
c)   Semillon accounts for less than one per cent of most total vineyard plantings.
d)   It can be drunk early or kept to age for 10, even 20 years.
e)   During fermentation it develops gloriously complex flavours without losing its freshness.

1.3   Styles

There are two styles of Semillon - young ones and older ones:

a)   In its youth, this wine can smell of grass or gooseberries or lime but without any great depth. At the age of about two, it closes up and becomes downright unpleasant.
b)   At around six years of age (or less in warmer regions), it begins to develop into a rich, golden wine like no other.
c)   Smelling and tasting like lemon curd on toast, it feels light in the mouth, despite those bold flavours, leaving behind a deliciously fresh tang.
d)   High acidity often makes young Semillons taste tart, but is the magic ingredient that makes them live for years.

TASK 12D

- Key in the following text.
- Save as 'Sales Salaries'.
- Edit as suggested.
- Apply the variable column layout as displayed.
- Resave.

DOCUMENT 1:

SALES SALARIES

t r s A recent survey by (marketing) and (sales) recruitment firms suggest tough competition in the computer industry has put sales and marketing salaries under pressure.

One reliable source states that the average basic salary for a sales representative in the IT sector has fallen from £25,000 to £18,630 in the space of *four* ~~three~~ years. *NP* The report says high levels of commission/bonuses continue to form a significant part of the pay package for most IT sales executives.

Replace "IT" with Information Technology

The survey found that an average £11,400 is paid over in commission, a figure nearly double that of other sectors. IT sales directors, with an average basic of ~~£37,000~~, still came out as top earners in sales. *£43,000*

The last two years have seen the emergence of telesales and telemarketing as strong growth areas for jobs. Basic salaries here averaged £11,290. Two-thirds of companies sampled said they paid a contributory pension to the sales executives. *have always*

DOCUMENT 2:

Remove Underlining after Saving; highlighter & Save again

THIRD PARTY MAINTENANCE

The computer maintenance market has faced a change in direction in recent years, as trends within the wider IT industry - such as falling hardware costs - have pushed profit margins even lower.

Until ~~a few~~ *sick* years ago, maintenance companies could make a comfortable living by charging a yearly fee of

10 per cent of equipment cost. Now that the ~~average~~ PC can be bought for less than £1000, the resulting 10 per cent maintenance charge barely covers the engineer's petrol expenses for one long distance site visit.

Add to this the pressures of having to provide customers with a single source of maintenance for a whole range of manufacturers, and the ever-present possibility

of newcomers buying up market share by offering rock bottom rates, and it is easy to see why established computer maintenance firms are keen to develop new ways of selling their wares.

According to one source, 80 per cent of company's overheads relate to labour and transport. The cost of (new and replacement) *t r s* parts is no longer a significant factor.

* Make a Page break. Copy document(s) overleaf. Change Column layout from 2/3 to 3/L. Number Pages 9 and 10.

TASK 9B

- Create the following financial statement.
- Use the layout as displayed.
- Save as 'A Trader'.
- Print one copy.

	£	£		£
Trading Account of A. Trader				
for year ended 31 December 19. .				
Opening stock		25 200	Sales	90 000
Purchases	60 480		*Less* Returns	240
Less Returns	1 080		Net turnover	89 760
		59 400		
		84 600		
Less Closing stock		18 720		
Cost of stock sold		65 880		
Gross profit		23 880		
		£89 760		£89 760

TASK 12C

- Key in the following text.
- Highlight text and use your WP column command to apply a three-column format.
- Save as 'Computer Maintenance'.

Document 3:

Computer Maintenance

With hardware firmly relegated to the ranks of commodity items, user attention is now firmly focused on software. If a piece of hardware breaks down, users expect it to be fixed ~~quickly and with the~~ immediately.

~~minimum of fuss.~~ Maintenance companies have taken note of these developments and are no longer arriving on site, counting the number of machines and delivering a quote

based on equipment cost. They ~~are~~ now ~~for more likely to~~ take a healthy interest in what applications those machines are running, and how critical these applications are to the running of the business.

Maintenance suppliers are attempting to distinguish between the maintenance of a server running mission-critical applications and that of a PC running the word processing package.

Maintenance agreements are devised that are tailor-made for each company. If a machine is running an application, spare parts might need to be stored on site and a lower response time guaranteed.

Document 4:

Assessing Service Levels

Whatever the individual claims, the issue of maintenance company size is something which the user needs to assess independently and with careful reference to its own needs. Obviously, the company needs to be of sufficient critical mass to maintain its service level

promises while still being flexible and responsive to the client's needs.

A comprehensive approach is needed for larger clients. IT managers need a service partner who will cover their whole system, not just half of it.

They need to be able to say 'I expect you to fix this situation today.' They require a service provided to deliver multivendor support to their business regardless of the technology involved.

Yet despite sales pitches littered with assurances of unique, tailor-made and

premium service, there are market similarities between what the main players offer. ~~For example,~~ the average UK response time appears to be about ~~four hours.~~ three

Everyone agrees that on-site service is a must. If the piece of equipment cannot be fixed speedily then clients should be

provided with a replacement part of machine until the problem has been sorted out.

The client should not be bothered with the details of the breakdown and more importantly the breakdown's effect on the running of the business should be kept to a minimum.

Create a page break. Copy edited documents to second page. Change font to: Courier (12) remove column format. Print this page once.

TASK 9C

- Create the following trading account.
- Use the layout suggested in the guidelines.
- Save as 'Sunshine Boutique'.
- Print one copy.

Sunshine Boutique (E. Rawlinson)
Trading Account for year ending 31 December 19. .

19. .		£	£	19. .		£
31 Dec.	Opening stock		12 820	31 Dec.	Sales	211 200
	Purchases	148 625			Less Returns	1 200
	Add Carriage in	675				
		———			Net turnover	210 000
		149 300				
	Less Returns	2 120				
		———				
			147 180			
	Total stock available		160 000			
	Less Closing stock		32 500			
			———			
	Cost of stock sold		127 500			
	Wages		27 500			
			———			
	Cost of sales		155 000			
	Gross profit		55 000			
			———			
			£210 000			£210 000

TASK 12B

- Key in the following text.
- Edit as suggested.
- Highlight text and use your WP column command to apply a two-column format.
- Save as 'Program'.
- Print one copy.

Stages of Programming

In the process of ~~producing the necessary instructions~~ making up a program [the following u.c. stages can be recognised]

b. Planning the method of solution.

a. Understanding the problem.

c. Developing the method using suitable methods and notations.

d. Typing the instructions into the computer in a programming language.

f. Documenting all the work involved in producing the program. This documentation will be developed stage by stage.

e. Testing the subprograms separately as they are each produced and finally testing the program as a whole.

If during testing the program an error is discovered then it is important to go back to the earlier stages in order to correct the error. If the error comes from misunderstanding the problem, it will probably be better to start again from the beginning. [Understanding the N.P. problem: [The programmer needs to know exactly what the program is required to do and normally works from a program specification.

This program specification is normally part of a 'system specification', which defines the whole system, of which the program may be only a small part. For example, the program might just be one of a suite of programs for use in a particular application.

Broadly speaking the program specification will define the inputs and processing outputs required. A good specification will normally specify what processing is needed by giving the exact relationship between (outputs) and (the inputs) from which they are derived rather than prescribing how the program should be written.

Ragged margin and use hyphenation facility

TASK 9D

- Create the following profit and loss account.
- Use the layout as displayed.
- Save as 'Rawlinson'.
- Print one copy.

<table>
<tr><td colspan="6" align="center">Sunshine Boutique (E. Rawlinson)</td></tr>
<tr><td colspan="6" align="center">Profit and Loss Account for year ending 31 December 19. .</td></tr>
<tr><td>19. .</td><td></td><td>£</td><td>19. .</td><td></td><td>£</td></tr>
<tr><td>31 Dec.</td><td>Salaries</td><td>7 500</td><td>31 Dec.</td><td>Gross profit</td><td>55 000</td></tr>
<tr><td></td><td>Administration Expenses</td><td>2 100</td><td></td><td>Discount Received</td><td>3 750</td></tr>
<tr><td></td><td>Light and Heat</td><td>3 400</td><td></td><td>Commissions Earned</td><td>7 750</td></tr>
<tr><td></td><td>Rent and Rates</td><td>8 250</td><td></td><td></td><td>66 500</td></tr>
<tr><td></td><td>Insurance</td><td>2 250</td><td></td><td></td><td></td></tr>
<tr><td></td><td>Advertising</td><td>6 200</td><td></td><td></td><td></td></tr>
<tr><td></td><td>Carriage Out</td><td>500</td><td></td><td></td><td></td></tr>
<tr><td></td><td></td><td>30 200</td><td></td><td></td><td></td></tr>
<tr><td></td><td>Net profit</td><td>36 300</td><td></td><td></td><td></td></tr>
<tr><td></td><td></td><td>£66 500</td><td></td><td></td><td>£66 500</td></tr>
</table>

TASK 12A

- Key in the following text.
- Highlight text and use your WP column command to apply a two-column format.
- Save as 'Communications'.

Communications between the printer and the PC obviously consist largely of print job data sent from the computer to the printer. However, communications flow in the other direction, as well. The printer also sends signals back to the PC for the purpose of flow control, that is, to inform the computer when to stop sending data and when to resume. The printer typically has an internal memory buffer that is smaller than the average print job and can only handle a certain amount of data at a time. As pages are actually printed, the printer purges data from its buffer and signals the PC to continue transmitting. This is commonly called handshaking. The hand-shaking protocols used for this communication are dependent on the port used to connect the printer to the PC.

TASK 9E

- Create the following balance sheet.
- Use the layout as displayed.
- Save as 'Balance Sheet'.
- Print one copy.

Sunshine Boutique (E. Rawlinson)
Balance Sheet as at 31 December 19. .

Fixed assets:	£	£	£	Capital:	£	£
Goodwill			4 000	At start		56 000
Land and buildings			48 000	*Add* Net profit	36 300	
Fixtures and fittings			3 600	*Less* Drawings	13 600	
Motor vehicles			11 000			22 700
			66 600			78 700
Current assets:						
Stock		32 500				
Debtors	2 560			Long-term liabilities:		
Less Provision	320			Mortgage		15 000
				Current liabilities:		
		2 240		Creditors	12 350	
Cash at bank		4 800		Wages due	150	
Cash in hand		60				12 500
			39 600			
			£106 200			£106 200

Guidelines

1. Column Styles

The default column style is a single column; i.e. the text flows on one line from the left to the right margin and wraps to the next line unless adjusted by the hitting of the Return key, or the use of the Tab key etc. WP software provides a facility where the text can be divided into two, three or more columns, or have a variety of columnar arrangements on one page. Word, for example, will require the insertion of section breaks in order to change from a two-columnar to three-columnar effect. A facility is also included in the software for creating lines.

2. Creating Two Columns

How you create two columns in the middle of a document depends very much on the software you are using. However, it is generally easier to key in all the text first, then highlight the part of the text that you wish to put into columns and then apply the column facility. If you switch on two columns at the appropriate point and then type, you may have a problem as the previous text will also take on a two-column format.

3. Dividers

You may have a facility on your software to insert dividers between different parts of the page. However, if this is not the case then just draw a line using the drawing tools. You may need to insert some hard spaces in order to place the lines neatly.

TASK 9F

- Create the following flow chart.
- Use the layout indicated.
- Save as 'Flow of Data'.
- Print one copy.

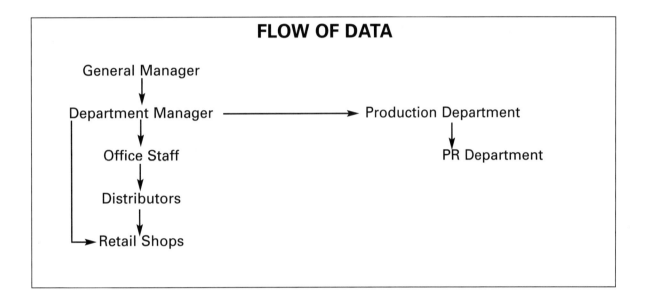

Unit 12

Columns

Dividers

TASK 9G

- Create the following organisation chart.
- Use arrows to indicate hierarchical structure.
- Save as 'Hickey'.
- Print one copy.

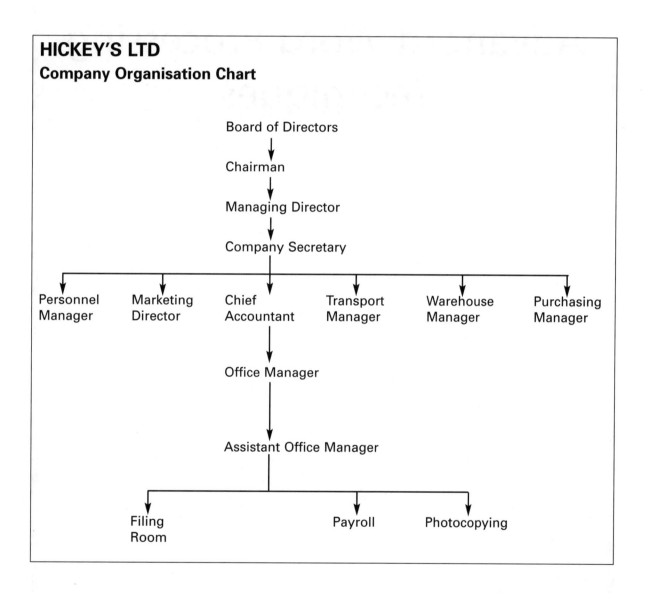

HICKEY'S LTD
Company Organisation Chart

Board of Directors

Chairman

Managing Director

Company Secretary

Personnel Manager | Marketing Director | Chief Accountant | Transport Manager | Warehouse Manager | Purchasing Manager

Office Manager

Assistant Office Manager

Filing Room | Payroll | Photocopying

SECTION THREE

Advanced Word Processing Techniques

Unit 10

Legal Documents

Advertisements

Display Work

TASK 11F

- Set up the letters described below, amalgamating stored blocks, as instructed.

i   Mr John Smith of 23 John St Bundoran Co Donegal
ii Ms Jackie Scales The Laurels River Road Clonmel Co Tipperary
iii Mr Mike O'Toole of Windy Ridge Crookhaven Co Cork

Use today's date in all letters and the topic heading (Guidelines for future assignments) should be centred and emboldened.

Mr Smith's Letter:

The first paragraph ~~will begin with the sentence~~ consists of; "On behalf of my staff and myself, I want to extend warm congratulations to you on your appointment as Branch Manager of 'Tandew'.

The second paragraph begins with: "I would like to draw your attention to the following established practices: Continue with files Design 1 and 2 amalgamated as one paragraph. Do not include emboldened headings of either file.

File: Design 4 is to be used as the third paragraph followed by the sentence: "Wishing you every good luck in your new appointment and assuring you of our support".

Conclude with: Yours Sincerely John Clinton General Manager. Leave room for Mr Clinton's signature.

Ms Scales's Letter:

Thank her for her recent letter. Files: Design 2 and 6 will form the second paragraph.

Conclude with the remark "If further information becomes available, I will keep you posted"

Mr Clinton will sign this letter also.

Mike O'Toole letter

Mr Clinton sends a covering letter on to Mr O'Toole with his new electronic typewriter.

He thanks Mr O'Toole for his business and wishes him well with his new IBM Personal wheelwriter. He wants to draw Mr O'Toole's attention to the sentiments expressed in Design 5 and 6. Mr Clinton signs the letter.

Guidelines

1. Legal Documents

Prior to word processing, there were three stages to producing a legal document:
Draft-typed with wide margins, treble-line spacing.
Fair copy — corrected draft in double-line spacing.
Engrossment — final copy for signature, usually produced on a 'parchment substitute' material.

The **engrossment** was usually typed in double-line spacing, without punctuation and with key words and phrases in capitals or spaced capitals.

Underlining was used and lines were inserted at the ends of clauses to prevent fraudulent additions.

Except for dates of Acts of Parliament, house numbers and clause numbers, **figures** were not used. Since the draft was considered a rough copy, **figures** and **abbreviations** were used.

With the advent of the word processor, drafts, fair copies and engrossments are rarely produced. **Standard Paragraphs** are stored, recalled and 'personalised' so that documents are 'engrossed' without the draft and fair copies being necessary. Additional copies are **photocopied** or printed.

The **Endorsement** is typed on the outside back sheet of a legal document, so at a glance, it can be seen what the document is and who the 'parties' are.

```
DATED
                                             2001
                    Mr C Clarke
                        TO
                    Ms S Smith
                   CONVEYANCE
OF
Freehold Property situated and known as 234
Coburg Street in the County of CORK

Dawson & Son Ltd
Galway
```

2. Advertisements

The descriptions in advertisements should be concise and the information clearly stated. Use emboldening, closed capitals and vary the font type and size for emphasis.

TASK 11E

• Key in the blocks below, saving under the specified names.

File : Design 1

Sizes. Standard-size forms should be used, as it is more economical to do so, and handling, filing and copying are simplified.

File: Design 2

Types of paper. The quality of paper used should be appropriate to requirements. Consideration should be given to such things as frequency of handling, storage needs, conditions under which forms are completed, and prestige requirements.

File : Design 3

Identification. There should be a brief, self-explanatory title; copies should be identified by different colours or bold symbols; serial numbering may be required for internal check purposes.

File : Design 4

Common information. If two forms are used in conjunction with each other, the common information should be in the same sequence and position.

File: Design 5

Vertical spacing. There should be adequate space off each item of entry, e.g. an invoice should have enough spaces to cover the normal number of items ordered. If a typewriter is being used in recording data on a form, consideration must be given to the normal vertical spacing requirements of the machine.

File: Design 6

Columns. The length of column headings should be tailored to the width required by the information to be entered in the column.

3. Display Work

Various techniques can be used to effectively display data:
Line spacing can be varied.
Various styles of capitals can be used e.g. spaced or closed.

Spaced Caps: I M P E R I A L   H O T E L
(3 spaces between words when using spaced caps)

Closed Caps: IMPERIAL HOTEL

Both **underlining** and **emboldening** can be used for emphasis:
<u>Market Day</u> this Thursday in **CLONMEL**

Correct use of **margins**: indent from left and right margins to allow for clip art etc.
Use centred alignment where appropriate for headings.

Example of a display using Clip Art

R A I L T O U R S   I R E L A N D

Great <u>Day</u> Tours **2000**

Only £19 <u>per person</u>

Departs Daily: Mon–Sat

• Advance Booking Essential
• Reserved Seats and Host
• Coach Tours to Avoca
• Stop in Village

---

4. Styles: Meetings

To display information about meetings:
Use blocked or centred style.
Allow one clear line for an effective design, particularly below headings.
Use capitals, spaced capitals, underlining or emboldening for emphasis where appropriate on headings.

TASK 11D

- Set up the documents below amalgamating stored blocks, as instructed.
- Allow 2" of space in all letters before the second paragraph, for the inclusion of a photograph.
- The auctioneer will sign all the letters.

The Auctioneer: Mr Tom Hassett, Riverbank, Ardmore, Co Waterford is involved in the selling of all these houses.

Mr John Twomey of 'Inniscarra View', Bundoran, Co Donegal is to be sent a letter which will be composed of three paragraphs: PROP6-8.

Ms Rita Whelan is looking out for a Victorian residence. She is sent a letter informing her of such a property now for sale. The stored paragraphs to be used in this letter are: PROP1, 2 and 5. Ms Whelan is currently resident at 67 Wellington Road, Cork.

Write to Mr Paul Norton of Belvelly, Cobh, Co Cork. Notify him of the property described under PROP3. Tell him what it consists of by including paragraphs PROP9 and 8.

A letter is sent by the auctioneers to Ms Sheila Ryan of Norwood Court, Rochestown Road, Cork. PROP3 forms the opening paragraph. Tell Ms Ryan that a lovely family home, in mint condition, spectacular 1/3 landscaped site with panoramic view of Harbour and City is listed for sale. It has an ultra modern layout, making maximum availability of the breathtaking views.

TASK 10A

- Set up the following will as displayed.
- Save as 'Last Will'.

<u>THIS IS</u>
<u>T H E   L A S T   W I L L   A N D   T E S T A M E N T</u>
of me
<u>CHARLES CLARKE</u> of Lee View, Fermoy in the County of Cork which I made this
day of   two thousand

    1. <u>I HEREBY REVOKE</u> all former wills and testamentary dispositions heretofore
made by me and <u>DECLARE</u> this to be my last
WILL_____
    2. <u>I APPOINT</u> my wife Rita Willis of Lee View, Fermoy, aforesaid and Jim Wright of
Cork Road, Mallow in the County of Cork to be the Executors of this my
WILL_____
    3. <u>I GIVE DEVISE AND BEQUATH</u> all my estate and effects whatsoever and where-
soever subject to the payment thereout of my just debts funeral and testamentary
expenses into my wife the said, Rita Willis absolutely

_____
    4. I DIRECT that my body shall be cremated and that these ashes shall be scat-
tered wheresoever my wife shall direct_____
    5. IN WITNESS whereof I have hereunto set my
hand_____

SIGNED by the said Charles Willis)
as and for his last Will and testament   )
in our joint presence and by us in his   )
presence:-   )

TASK 11C

- Key in the following blocks of text, saving individually under the specified filenames.

PROP 1

Attractive Victorian residence situated close to a castle and standing on 1.5 acres of mature private gardens and enjoying an all-weather manage. Also included is a guest cottage and an excellent range of outbuildings.

PROP 2

Contains: Three reception rooms, sunroom, fully-fitted kitchen, utility room, five bedrooms, two bathrooms, guest toilet.

PROP 3

I want to draw your attention to an exceptional property that has come on to the market. It consists as follows:

PROP 4

Resume: Hall, Livingroom, Diningroom, Kitchen, 3 bedrooms, Bathroom, enclosed rear yard, priced to sell.

PROP 5

Guest cottage with sittingroom, kitchenette, two bedrooms, Bathroom, two stables, tackroom, lofted store.

PROP 6

In accordance with your instructions, I have been looking out for the type of property in which you were interested in. The following has just come on-stream:

PROP 7

Expertly-built 4-Bedroomed, detached home on a lovely landscaped 0.4-acre site.

PROP 8

Absolutely spectacular condition throughout. Must be seen to appreciate what's on offer. Central location adjacent to schools, shops, churches, etc.

PROP 9

Resume: porch, Hall, Lounge, Dining, Kitchen, Sun Lounge, 3 Bedrooms, en-suite Bathroom, garage ready for conversion. Dual heating, tarmacadamed forecourt.

TASK 10B

- Set up the following agreement; use double-line spacing.
- Save as 'Clarke'.

A N   A G R E E M E N T made the day of One thousand nine hundred and BETWEEN CHARLES CLARKE of Lee View, Fermoy in the County of Cork (hereinafter called 'the Manufacturer' which expression shall where the context admits include the Manufacturer's executors and administrators and assigns) of the one part and JOHN LONG of Fermoy in the County of Cork (hereinafter called 'the Agent' which expression shall where the context admits include the Agent's executors and administrators and assigns or successors in business as the case may be) of the other part

WHEREBY IT IS MUTUALLY AGREED as follows

The Manufacturer grants to the Agent in consideration of the payment by the Agent of a non-returnable AGENCY FEE. of Three thousand pounds (the receipt whereof the Manufacturer hereby acknowledges) the sole and exclusive right to sell in the UNITED KINGDOM ONLY all items of sugar confectionery ordered for resale from the Manufacturer by the Agent on the following terms

LETTER 3

BUSINESS

Today's date

Ms Rita Moore
The Mall
Youghal
Co Cork

Dear Ms Moore

REP1

We note that you were not completely satisfied with last month's delivery.

ORDER2 — (Amend "this order" to "this new order")

INV1

In view of your dissatisfaction, £500 is deducted from amount due.

COMP1

LETTER 4

BUSINESS

Today's date

Mr John Kilgrew
North Main St
Cork

Dear Sir

REP2

We are happy to inform you that a consignment was delivered today. Your order, detailed below is top-of-the-range.

Dell Dimension 466DL	Intel 66MHz Pentium Processor	525MB Hard Drive	Trio 2MB Graphics Card	£1,049 (ex VAT)
Dell Dimension XPS P75	Intel 75MHz Pentium Processor	600MB Hard Drive	256KB Cache	£1,339 (ex VAT)
Dell Dimension XPK	Intel 80MHz Pentium Processor	650MB Hard Drive	Mid-Sized Desktop Chassis	£1,234 (ex VAT)

All Computers have 8MB RAM, 3.5 Diskette Drives and include 14" SVGA Monitors.

INV1

COMP2

TASK 10C

• Create the following advertisement; display it attractively.

For Sale: NEARLY NEW PERSONAL FAX MACHINE

Clear and simple to use. On-hook dialling and a 10 sheet document feed
ensure effective use on this business machine. 60 speed dials. Stores up to
60 of your most frequently used numbers in the memory and recall at the
touch of a button. Would suit small business or home user.

Price £295.

Please reply to BOX 1559 or telephone 021 45454567

TASK 11B

- Set up the following letters recalling the stored documents, as indicated.

- Set the top and bottom margins at 2.54 cm, the left margin at 3 cm, and the right with a ragged margin.

LETTER 1

BUSINESS

Today's date

Ms Jane Sorenson
Baker's Row
London SW1

Dear Ms Sorenson

REP1

I note that these are as follows:

SUPPLIER	PROCESSOR	MEMORY	HARD DISK	PRICE (ex VAT)
Apple	DX 2 (50 MHz)	4 MB	170	915
Toshiba	486 DX-66 (66 MHz)	8 MB	250	1050
Siemens	Intel 80486 33 MHz)	8 MB	510	1195
Fujitsu	486 DX50 16 MHz)	2 MB	20	930

ORDER2

I hope this delivery meets with your approval.

COMP1

LETTER 2

BUSINESS

Today's date

Mr John Fitzpatrick
Menloe Gardens
Blackrock
Cork

Dear Sir

REP2

ORDER1

Unless, we hear from you, this order will be shipped on the 10 of next month.

We appreciate your regular custom over the last number of years.

COMP2

TASK 10D

• Create the following advertisement; display it attractively.

For Sale: TOP QUALITY CD-Rs

MULTISPEED. These multispeed CD-Rs can be used with the latest CD-R
recorders.

Playback. Once recorded they can be played back on standard CD-Rom, CD-
ROM, CD-ROM XA, CD-Audio or CD-Interactive drives. LIFETIME GUARAN-
TEE. Minimum archival life of 100 years.

TASK 11A

- Key in the following 8 blocks, saving separately under the specified filenames. Turn overleaf and assemble the letters, as directed.

---

1. Kayser's Computing
   Tourist House
   41 Grand Parade
   Cork
   Tel. 021 4274402

   Save as BUSINESS.

2. Further to your recent telephone call, requesting a supply of varied computer products.

- Save as REP1.

3. Thank you for your recent memo regarding products that we have now in stock.

- Save as REP2.

4. Unfortunately, due to the phenomenal demand for our products, resulting from our promotion at the Windows Show in the RDS, we will be unable to fulfil your order until early next month.

- Save as ORDER1.

5. We are happy to inform you that this order is being shipped today.

- Save as ORDER2.

6. I am enclosing an invoice for these goods.

- Save as INV1.

7. Yours sincerely
   <u>Sales Manager</u>
   KAYSER'S COMPUTING

- Save as COMP1.

8. Yours faithfully
   <u>Purchasing Officer</u>
   KAYSER'S COMPUTING

- Save as COMP2.

TASK 10E

- Display a notice of an annual general meeting and agenda.

DOUGLAS GARDEN CLUB

18 September 2001

The Annual General Meeting of the Douglas Garden Club will be held in the Community Centre on Monday next, 25 September 2000, at 8 pm.

A G E N D A

1. Apologies
2. Minutes of the last meeting
3. Matters arising
4. Chairman's Annual Report
5. Secretary's Annual Report
6. Treasurer's Annual Report followed by discussion
7. Election of Officers for the coming year – Nominations must be submitted prior to Meeting
8. Discuss trip to Chelsea Flower Show – fund-raising progress to date
9. Any other business

S Shaw
Hon Secretary

Guidelines

1. Stored Paragraphs

Blocks of text may be saved separately and then recalled individually, as required, using the insert file feature of your WP software.

TASK 10F

- Display the following notice on A5 paper.

SECRETARY URGENTLY REQUIRED

Secretary urgently required by Personnel Officer of a large multi-national.

WP skills <u>essential</u> — Salary negotiable.

Apply in confidence to:

    Harcourt & Son

    Solicitors

    Main St

    Arklow

    Co Wicklow

Unit 11

Stored Paragraphs

TASK 10G

- Display the following notice on A5 paper.
- Save as 'Cardiac Unit MW'.

_A C C O M M O D A T I O N   R E Q U I R E D_

Two-bedroomed _self-contained_ flat required by responsible family with one child.

Ground floor <u>essential</u>.

Rent **reasonable**.

Good <u>references</u> supplied.

Apply to:

    Rita

    Cardiac Unit

    Bon Secours

    Cork

TASK 10J

- Create the following document.

- Set up features as follows:

  Margins
  Indentation
  Hanging paragraph
  Line spacing.

- Save as 'Proofing MW'.

Proofing a Document

which help you to correct errors

Within Windows, there are three important tools. The spelling command finds misspelled words. *TEXT*

1½" MARGINS

[The Grammar command checks for important categories of grammatical flaws in your document and suggests possible improvements *CORRECTIONS*.] The Thesaurus provides lists of synonyms for words you select in your document.

INDENT 2" from both sides

Saving your Changes

HANGING PARAGRAPHS

It is important to remember *KEEP IN MIND* when you're editing a document that your changes are made to the copy stored *OF THE DOCUMENT CURRENTLY* on the disk. Therefore, its important to save your work when you are editing an existing document. If you switch off your computer, your changes will be lost.

NP

1" MARGINS

lc Remember, save your work every five minutes. Don't forget to save and exit your work [When you are finished with your word processor for the time being] 2

double spacing

TASK 10H

- Create the following document.
- Fully justify and indent by .5" the second and third paragraphs, at both the left and right margins.
- Save as 'Mobile Phone MW'.
- Print one copy on A4 portrait paper.

FRESH COMPETITION IN MOBILE PHONE MARKET

Consumers should have the choice of another mobile phone operator before Christmas following a Supreme Court ruling which has paved the way for fresh competition in the fast growing mobile phone market:

> In an unanimous decision, the supreme Court allowed an appeal by the telecom regulator against a High Court order quashing her decision to aware the third mobile phone license to the US-Irish consortium, Meteor.

> The Supreme Court found a claim by rival bidder, Orange that the regulator had displayed bias and some form of xenophobic prejudice against the British operator, were "entirely misconceived" and the suggestion "strains credulity to breaking point".

"There was not a scintilla of evidence that the director or any member of her staff or any of the consultants retained by her had any interest whatever in pecuniary or other nature in the outcome of the tender process", the court ruled.

TASK 10I

- Create the following document.
- Centre and embolden the heading.
- Set up a hanging paragraph .5" for the body of the document.
- Save as 'Mortgages MW'.
- Print one copy on A5 landscape paper.

House prices still surge despite rising mortgages

House prices continue to surge despite rising mortgage rates. The rate of increase in the cost of houses during the first four months of the year has outstripped last year. House values across Ireland grew by 6.6 per cent compared to 4.6 per cent for the same period in 1999.

Prices outside Dublin continue to rise faster than those in the capital and are driving the index. This reflects the growth of satellite towns and also higher prices in Cork and other urban areas.

Although mortgage rates have increased there has been no let up in the demand for houses and only a small increase in supply.